Glimpses of the Life of Our Lord

By

W. G. Blaikie, D. D.

PROFESSOR OF APOLOGETICS AND OF PASTORAL
THEOLOGY IN THE NEW COLLEGE, EDINBURGH.

LONDON

HODDER AND STOUGHTON,

27, PATERNOSTER ROW.

1876

Republished by Laus Deo Books.

Cover photo courtesy of Paul McGowan and CC0 Public Domain

ISBN: 9781520761831

PREFACE

The aim of this little book is devotional and practical. The author desires to help earnest hearts in their endeavors after the Christian life; and believes that for this end no fitter means can be found than the devout consideration of the inner life of our Lord.

CONTENTS

HIS DEVOTION TO THE FATHER'S WORK

"Wist ye not that I must be about my Father's business?"
— Luke 2.49

It is surely not without a purpose that, in St. Luke's narrative, the memorable saying of Christ's childhood stands midway between two statements of His growth and progress. A few verses before (ver. 40) we read that "the child Jesus grew and waxed strong in the spirit, and the grace of God was upon him;" a few verses after (ver. 52), "Jesus increased in wisdom and stature, and in favour with God and man." If there be a purpose in this arrangement, must it not be to teach us that it was as the result of the process referred to in the earlier verse that the saying in the temple was uttered; while, as the result of the continued progress noticed in the other verse, the whole life followed that is recorded in this Gospel. The direction in which He was growing is significantly indicated in the memorable utterance of the Child, "I must be about my Father's business;" the mature fruit of the process is displayed to us in the whole transactions of His public life, beautifully summed up in the words of His closing prayer, "I have glorified thee on the earth: I have finished the work which thou gavest me to do."

At the very least, the words of St. Luke imply that, in some sense, the human nature of the man Christ Jesus advanced and ripened by gradual steps. We are apt to be blinded to this fact by the dazzling glory of His Divine nature. The more that we love and honor our Lord, the more do our hearts fill with His infinite majesty, and the less are we disposed to think of His having ever had any, even sinless, imperfection. The more that we feel what we owe to Him who loved us, and who washed us from our sins in His own blood, the more are we disposed to prostrate ourselves before His throne; and no song seems equal to the occasion save that which gives to the Lamb that was slain all "power, and riches, and wisdom, and strength, and honour, and glory, and blessing."

But this is only one side of the twofold nature of Jesus, and it cannot be right to allow the higher to conceal the lower. St. Luke's words refer to the lower, or human side, and they indicate a fourfold growth — physical, intellectual, moral, and spiritual. Slightly changing the order, to bring out the climax, we find Jesus growing physically — "in stature;" intellectually — "in wisdom;" morally — "in favour with man;" spiritually — "in favour with God." The first member of this enumeration is easily believed; but, step by step, the difficulty of belief increases, and when we read that Jesus grew in favor with God, our difficulty is at the greatest. Yet His soul, as much as His body, was part of that human nature which He took on Him; and, sinless though it was, it followed the same law of gradual increase. The qualities that made Him "fairer than the children of men" reached their maturity by degrees, as the oak attains its strength, or the peach its flavor. Year by year the human nature unfolded itself, and its beauty increased, reaching its climax, as we may believe, when the voice burst from the sky, "This is my beloved Son, in whom I am well pleased."

In the growth of human nature, the process is partly involuntary, and partly the result of will and effort. The growth of our lower or animal nature is almost wholly involuntary; but the higher the part in which the growth takes place, the more scope and need is there for conscious effort. It is not by taking thought that we can add a cubit to our stature; the hair grows, the nails push forward, whether we will or no. But in the higher departments of our nature there is no progress without exercise and effort. "Herein do I exercise myself," says St. Paul, describing the working of his inner life, "to have always a conscience void of offence toward God, and toward man." "Gird up the loins of your minds," says St. Peter, in a similar connection, "be sober, and hope to the end."

When, therefore, we read of the gradual ripening of the moral and spiritual nature of Jesus, we cannot suppose that it was a quite passive and involuntary process; it must have been the result of much holy will and effort. Sinless though He was, and incapable of sin, His high human attainments could have ripened only by degrees, and not without much painstaking on His part, and many a prayer that God's will might be done. His consecration to His Father's business, for example — the attainment with which we are now specially concerned — must have been, in its maturest and completest form, the result of much soul-exercise. Many persons, if they think at all how He attained this consecration, fancy that it came to Him without effort, or without any use of means. We believe, on the contrary, that it was the ripe fruit of a lifelong process, the earliest stage of which was indicated in the question put to His mother in the temple; and the last in His sublime words in Gethsemane, "Not my will, but thine be done."

The question in the temple, "How is it that ye sought me? Wist ye not that I must be about my Father's business?" shows a singular combination of the simplicity of a child with the deep soul-exercise of a saint. There is a child's astonishment in the form of the question; He never thought they would have been agitated about Him. A child wonders that others should be troubled when he is not troubled — wonders that others should not take the same view of the matter as he takes himself. But of what profound experience is this question a proof! Already the Father's business has wholly absorbed Jesus. It has swallowed up every other interest of His young heart. Aaron's rod has swallowed up all the rods of the magicians. And yet in this, Jesus seems unconscious of anything unusual or peculiar. It is with perfect frankness and simplicity He refers to it. It seems to Him so natural it should be so, that He wonders His mother should have had any other thought. "Wist ye not that I must be about my Father's business?"

The question implies that Mary knew something of the aims and feelings of Jesus, and therefore leads us to think of the intercourse they must have had together on such topics. It carries our thoughts to the nurture and admonition of the Lord in which she would bring Him up. And deeply interesting it is to consider what must have been the lessons which she would teach Him as soon as He was able to understand the Old Testament and its wonderful stories. It was her privilege to begin at a different point from all other mothers: she would not need to urge Him to give His heart to God; but, finding it with God already, would rather seek to develop and ripen the spirit of consecration, dwelling eagerly on the lives of those who had been remarkable for their devotion: of Enoch and Abraham, of Moses and Caleb and Joshua, of Samuel and David, and the long chain of godly men who, often in the face of bitter persecution, had worked so bravely for God in the world. And how apt a learner she must have found Him! How soon would His sympathies show themselves on the right side! How soon would the desire shape itself to take up the old banner, and continue the old work; to vindicate the Divine law, so shamefully trampled on; to draw men to love and honor the Father, and to walk in righteousness before Him all the days of their lives! How early must this have appeared to Jesus the grandest object for which men could live! How soon must all other modes and purposes of life — the pursuit of wealth, or of pleasure, or of fame, or even of wisdom and learning considered in, themselves — have dwindled into insignificance, compared with a life devoted to the glory of God and the highest good of man! It is plain that Jesus was possessed with such thoughts from His childhood; even at the age of twelve, the purpose to devote His life to the work of His Father had banished all rivals from His heart. Formally, Mary might continue to be His teacher, and never would her Son consciously make the office painful to her; yet how soon must she have felt that she had more need to learn of Him than He of her, whether the lessons might be lessons of the understanding or lessons of the heart. It has often been asked, Did the question in the temple imply a consciousness on the part of Jesus of His Messianic office in all its extent? Usually, it has been thought to imply that He already apprehended the truth of His relation to the Father, but that He had not yet arrived at a clear perception of all that was involved therein. Strange gleams of truth seem to have been flashing before Him; hints perhaps of what was coming; but his very eagerness in talking to the doctors seems to show that the whole truth had not yet been grasped.

Probably there were at least three stages in the self-dedication of Jesus.

1. The first — that announced in the temple — when, as a Child, he gave Himself, simply and frankly, to His Father's business. That business, in the first instance, was mainly to learn His will, as He had been learning it in the temple, and thereby prepare Himself for His active service. And it is not difficult to picture the first aspect under which the duty of serving His Father would present itself to His mind. Even ordinary children who get early grace are often, with their fresh moral instincts, more shocked than older men at the world's wickedness, and its daring rebellion against God's authority. What, then, to the holy, unpolluted instincts of Mary's Child, must have been the effect of His first intelligent survey of the ungodly world? The Psalmist's words will suggest the answer. "I beheld the transgressors, and was grieved." He would be shocked at what He saw, and eager to remedy it, but glad to sit at the feet of those who might have fuller knowledge of God's will, and how it was to be enforced on men. His sympathies would go forth right cordially with all who were making it their aim to induce men to follow the will of the Father. And here is a blessed example for every Christian child. See here, my child, these footprints, — the marks of a foot as small as your own. Look round

you, and observe how men are living. You see many regardless of the good God, and caring little for man; heedless of all the sin and suffering around them; heedless themselves, and teaching others to be heedless, alike of heaven and hell. On the other hand, you see a few trying to work with God and for God, trying to make the world better and brighter, trying to make sunshine in its shady places, and to turn this wilderness into the garden of the Lord. See how eagerly the heart of the Child Jesus goes with them! Will you, too, not throw in your lot with them and Him? Will you not say, "These people shall be my people, their work shall be my work, and their God my God"?

2. A further stage in the self-dedication of Jesus would be reached when, in view of the work and office of the prophets, He gave Himself, like them, to the public service of His Father. The work He was to do could not be merely that of a private individual; it must be that of an avowed, outstanding, public Ambassador. And this was no attractive post. The tombs of the prophets had indeed been built after they were dead; but in their lifetime they had been treated with opposition and scorn. Jerusalem, in a sense "the holy city," had become "the city that killed the prophets;" and so far from reposing in tranquility amid its sacred buildings as in a

congenial home, the prophets knew full well that nowhere were they more likely to meet with the malefactor's shameful death.

But braving everything of this kind, Jesus would cheerfully accept the prophet's *role*. And here is the great lesson for Christian ministers and all who are called publicly to the service of God. Shall we shrink from danger and dishonor when our blessed Master so unreservedly accepted a despised and hated function? Shall we bargain that if we are to be known as God's public servants, it shall only be in a well-provided church, amid all that is elegant and respectable? Would that among aspirants to the ministry there were more of the spirit that is ready, "by honour and dishonour, through evil report and good report," evermore to serve the Lord!

3. Lastly, the self-dedication of Jesus would completed when He gave Himself to the office of Messiah. But here we come into contact with elements which we are unable fully to comprehend. At what period of His life Jesus deliberately and consciously gave Himself to this office; whether He did so with the full knowledge at first of all its unexampled obligations; in

what manner, and at what time, his consciousness as a Man met the eternal purpose of His Godhead in the willing assumption of the functions of Messiah, are questions that are too deep for us, and with which therefore it is vain for us to perplex our minds.

But this we know full well, that the obligations of that office involved the most fearful ordeal ever set before the soul of man. The psalms that foretold Messiah's sufferings were dark and terrible in tone; the climax of His career, described in Isaiah's words as "making his soul an offering for sin," and "pouring his soul out unto death," was enough to shake any heart; and as the crisis drew near it is plain how deeply Jesus felt it, speaking as He did so plaintively of the coming hour and power of darkness, and of that unprecedented baptism by which He was so straitened till it should be, accomplished. To stand in the room of sinners, and be numbered with the transgressors; to be treated as if He had been guilty of the abominable thing which he hated; to have the sacrificing knife thrust into His bosom, and thus fulfill what was prefigured by all the blood of bulls and goats that had flowed from the beginning — who can estimate the horrors of such a position? Yet to this appalling office the Man Christ Jesus gave Himself on earth, as the Son had given Himself in heaven; and in spite of the recoil of flesh and blood, the quivering of the human nerve when touched by the sword of eternal justice, He endured patiently and meekly, till at last the word rung out, "It is finished!"

And who thinks the less of Jesus for that temporary recoil of flesh and blood? Was it not the touch of nature that makes us kin — that makes us feel that, with all His Divine glory, He was still a man? Who would have thought less of David Livingstone, or William Burns, or John Patteson, if for a moment their hearts had quivered at the thought of Africa, or China, or the South Sea Islands? Around the family hearth, amid the warmth of loving hearts, or in the society of like-minded friends, it would have been like a cold gust of the north wind to think chat they were going to part from all this, perhaps for ever. But the nobleness of their hearts would have been shown in their quickly displacing such thoughts by others — thoughts of the blessed cause to which they were devoting their lives, and of the call which God had given them to go forth on it; thoughts of all the blessing that would be carried to miserable multitudes, if success should crown their noble enterprise. So when for the moment the human soul of Christ recoiled from His sufferings, it was only that deeper thoughts might be called up to remove the shivering of the flesh — only that towards the Father's will He might place Himself in a profounder attitude of submission, and by anticipation refresh His soul with the joy that was set before Him, when at length His elect should be gathered to Him from the four winds of heaven.

The self-dedication of Jesus had thus, in all its stages, to be maintained by struggles against flesh and blood. From the visit in the temple at the age of twelve, when His Father's business laid such hold on Him, to the agony in Gethsemane immediately before His crucifixion, the inclinations of His human flesh had to be met and overcome by higher and nobler considerations. What, then, were these considerations? In what way was the spirit of self-dedication so unceasingly maintained?

1. In the first place, there was His profound submission to the Father's will. That will, to Jesus, was the only power that had a right to control the universe. It was the one grand, sovereign authority to which creation was subject. And that will did not represent sheer might that behoved to be obeyed, it represented all that was wise and holy and good. To resist it was not only infinite madness, but infinite wickedness. Let it lead Him where it might, Jesus could not dream of anything but

submission. Oh, rare and beautiful devotion, that can see nothing to be regarded save that will, even when it brings against Him all the pains of death and terrors of hell; even when Apollyon, with all his poisoned darts and hideous emissaries, is darkening the very sky, that can still calmly say, "I delight to do thy will, my God."

2. A second thing that sustained Christ was, His deep sense of what may be called the Messianic necessity. By the time He entered on His public ministry He fully understood the obligations of Messiah's work. It had become, indeed, the great business of His life. Into that work He now entered with the greatest enthusiasm. He was not merely at the point where He controlled His work, but at the much higher point where His work controlled Him. Hence His constant use of the word "must;" denoting, as it were, the categoric imperative under which He was placed. The view that began to dawn on Him in the temple, when He must be about His Father's business, gathered clearness and force as He went along. "I MUST work the work of him that sent me while it is day." "Other sheep I have, them also I must bring." "The Son of man must be delivered into the hands of sinful men." "This that is written MUST be accomplished." "As Moses lifted up the serpent in the wilderness, so must the Son of man be lifted up." "How

then shall the scripture be fulfilled that thus it MUST be?" No other thought can be entertained for a moment. Though the heavens were to fall, the whole functions of the Messianic office must be fulfilled to the end.

3. Thirdly, there was the view which Jesus had of the hideous nature of sin; its horrid antagonism to God, and to everything bright, sweet, and pure; its frightful sting and poison; its dreadful perversion of the soul and the life of man; its desolating power in this fair earth, like a lurid volcano in the heart of a paradise, scorching all that was green and fair as with streams of burning lava. To make an end of this sin is one of the great purposes for which He has come. But unless He shall receive its sting into His own person it cannot be destroyed. Once that sting is planted in Him, the monster will be comparatively powerless. Ought He then to shrink from the conflict? Must He not go forward bravely when this proud Philistine has to be destroyed?

4. Fourthly, There was the great love that surged in His heart: His sympathy with those He had come to save; the pain He felt in their pain; the joy He had in their joy. His twelve apostles, the family of Bethany, and His other

intimate friends were samples to Him of a great multitude round whom His heart-strings were twined, and for whom the prayer continually rose, "Father, I will that they be with me where I am." Shall He abandon those whom He loves with more than a woman's love, because He has come to the dregs of the cup, and its bitterness is overpowering? Shall His love be the love of summer only? shall it vanish at the approach of storms, when the responsibilities of His position are overwhelming? Never shall this be said of Him. Having loved His own that were with Him in the world, He loves them to the end.

5. Fifthly, there were some secondary views that must have contributed somewhat to the resolute self-dedication of Jesus. When one uses arguments in the form of proverbs or otherwise to commend steadfastness to others, we may believe that he has found them useful to himself. When Jesus taught the folly of beginning a tower without counting the cost, we may believe that He knew in His own case what such counting was, and was prepared for all that He had to meet as the result of his undertaking. When He rebuked indecision by the proverb, "No man having put his hand to the plough, and looking back, is fit for the kingdom of God," we may be sure He must have felt that it would

never do for Him to look back. When followers, excusing themselves on the ground of family duties, were told to let the dead bury their dead, we may conclude that Jesus was personally familiar with the counsel. All that He thus taught to others probably served at some time to give firmness to His own resolution, and keep His heart well knit for all that He was called to encounter.

6. Lastly, there was His habit of prayer. Communion with His Father was ever sought, as a means of strengthening His heart and confirming His resolutions. In the secret place of the Most High, He found His elixir of life, and He came forth from the presence chamber, rejoicing like a strong man to run a race.

But after all, we cannot know all that moved the soul of Jesus. We cannot fathom the workings of that Person which was God and man in one. But we see the blessed result. We see the process of consecration continued from first to last, from the temple to the cross, we see the grace steadily ripening, till his life is closed in with the glorious utterance, "I have finished the work which thou gavest me to do."

And surely this self-consecration of Jesus is the model for His followers. From this example and fountain has come all the grace that has at any time made noble lives and blessed service in the Christian Church. All that is glorious in the devotion of martyrs and missionaries, or in the lives of those who, in hospitals, ragged-schools, and filthy haunts of vice, have given themselves with gentle and patient love to seek and to save the lost, has had its inspiration here. The family of Jesus has no more conspicuous mark than this; it is the prominent feature of the many brethren who have been predestinated to be conformed to the image of the firstborn.

The more vividly we realize the self-dedication of Jesus, the more clearly do we see what, on a lower level, our lives ought to be. But, alas, where do we find this spirit? Side by side with this wonder of devotion to the work of the Father, and the good of men, how poor and miserable are most men's lives! How unworthy are we to bear Christ's name — with our self-indulgence, our meanness, our earthliness, our pride, our hatred! If Christ had left nothing but His example to influence us, lives much higher and nobler might surely have been expected of us.

But how much greater should be the influence when His sufferings were endured, not as an example only, but in our very room; when He bore our curse that we might receive His blessing; when He suffered our penalty that we might share His reward! Surely, if we are moved to no corresponding life — if we are wholly occupied with the interests of self and of this present world — if nothing is more out of our way than to deny ourselves and take up the cross and follow Him — there can be no pulse of Christ's life beating within us. May we hear His voice over our graves, calling, "Awake thou that sleepest, and arise from the dead!"

HIS DELIGHT IN THE FATHER'S WILL

"I delight to do thy will, O my God." — Psalm 40

There can be no reasonable doubt whose words these are. Even if the internal evidence were not sufficient, the reference to them in the tenth chapter of Hebrews shows conclusively that they are spoken by Jesus, "when he cometh into the world." And as there is no doubt about the speaker, so there is no ambiguity in the words. They indicate the great rule of Christ's earthly life; what He was continually thinking about, and planning to follow; what guided Him through the scenes of this world as truly and as constantly as a ship is guided by her helm. Further, they indicate the delight which it gave Him to follow this rule. There was no sense of pain in doing it; on the contrary, there was in it the pleasure which attends all free, spontaneous activity; nay, there was pleasure rising to delight, its highest elevation. Moreover, it is indicated that this was not an obscure or hidden feature of Christ's life; it was "written of Him in the volume of the book" — was foretold in the Old Testament and fulfilled in the New. This is a higher view of our Lord's human life than that which we have just considered. In our last chapter we saw His loyalty to duty; here His duty becomes His delight. In the last. His motto was *I must*; here it is *I will*. Conscience wedded to will; duty in combination with delight; the highest rule of life issuing in its purest enjoyment — how rare and how beautiful the sight! The devotion of the martyr blended with the delight of the enthusiast; the mortification of the lower nature swallowed up in the gratification of the higher; the pain of the flesh forgot in the joy of the spirit. Well may we say, Never man felt as this Man! Passages almost without number bear testimony to our Lord's profound regard for the Father's will. "I came down from heaven," He said, "not to do mine own will, but the will of him that sent me." And as this was the rule of His own life, so He desired that it should be the rule for others. He taught it to His disciples as one of their foremost petitions: "Thy will be done on earth as it is in heaven." He laid it down as the standard of judgment for the most solemn of all trials: "Not every one that saith unto me Lord, Lord, shall enter into the kingdom of heaven, but he that doeth the will of my Father which is in heaven." And far higher than any ties of fleshly relationship He counted the bond by which it united His followers to Himself: "For whosoever shall do the will of my Father who is in heaven, the same is my sister and brother and mother."

Of the delight which it gave Him to do God's will we have a memorable instance at the well of Jacob. When He arrived there, on His journey through Samaria, He seems to have been utterly exhausted; so that the disciples left Him at the well when they went into the city to buy bread. But when they returned, and offered Him food, He seemed indifferent to it, and told them that He had meat to eat which they knew not of. And what was that? "My meat," He said, "is to do the will of him that sent me, and to finish his work." The happiness of doing God's will, and accomplishing even a single part of His holy plan; the joy of stopping a guilty career and turning a lost sinner into the way of life; the triumphant feeling of the shepherd bearing back his lost sheep to the fold — sustained Him more than any meat or drink; the glad heart reacting on the exhausted body sent a fresh current through the veins. To Jesus this experience was meat and drink and sleep, and recreation combined; no gratification of the senses could have brought a tithe the refreshment. "I delight to do Thy will, O my God."

The thorough surrender of His own, will to the will of the Father was certainly one of the most remarkable things in the human life of Jesus. He who was in the form of God and thought it not robbery to be equal with God; He who from the beginning had been accustomed to have His will honored with all that reverence which the angels paid to God — entered as God's servant on a career in which He was to have no will of His own; a career, the very condition and necessity of which was, that in all things His will was to be ruled by the Father's. He deliberately entered on a mode of life in which He was to live out of Himself, and beyond Himself, as it were; regarding self neither as the rule nor the end of a single act or plan or effort, but invariably aiming at pleasing and serving another. Fancy a great emperor doing anything like this; fancy one of nature's kings — one evidently born to command, one who could form great plans, and summon hosts of men to realize them — becoming, for some reason, a menial servant; entering his own army or navy as a common soldier or sailor, and coming under the discipline of the service in its extremest rigor. Fancy him in the raging storm climbing to the masthead at the word of command, or in the raging battle creeping up the bristling battlement; never once thinking what he would like, guided every moment by the will of another. Perhaps such a case may be conceived; but there is one element in Christ's case that hardly can be thrown into this picture — the element of delight. We can hardly conceive an imperial spirit taking delight in this prostration of its own will. In the case of Jesus the delight was not affected but real; serving the Father was His meat and drink; pleasing God was His chiefest joy.

Our natural tendency is so different that, until we get Christ's spirit, we can hardly understand such a pleasure. Living for ourselves seems to come to us by instinct, so that we cannot think of any other course of life except as more or less constrained. How early the disposition shows itself in the child! Almost as soon as he can speak he learns to say, I want this, and I want that; rather, we should say, before he learns to speak, this is the language of his actions, the language of his eager looks and passionate tears, of the stretching of his little hands and the driving of his little feet. So early does the human will assert a claim to sovereignty, and demand, like Joseph's sheaf, that the other sheaves shall do obeisance around it. And usually, as man begins in childhood, he goes on in manhood, and he ends in old age. He learns, of course, as he gains experience of the world, that in certain directions he must restrain his inclinations, otherwise he will be in trouble in this world and in the next; but *so far as he safely can*, how much is the life of the man an extension of the life of the child: I want this, and I want that, and I shall have them if I can. How much is human life devoted to the advancement of its own interests and comforts, with now and then a little bit of tribute paid to a higher will, but paid reluctantly; paid because that will dare not be wholly disregarded; but not in the spirit of Jesus — not in the spirit of delight.

This delight of Jesus in doing the Father's will we see alike in what He did and in what He suffered.

It was the will of God that He should be subject to Joseph and Mary; that He should spend thirty years in the obscurity of Nazareth; that he should work as a carpenter, fashioning tables and chairs, spades and plows, for the rough Nazarenes; bullied by some of them, no doubt, and cheated by others; yet never a murmur of dissatisfaction escaped Him at so long and humbling a servitude.

It was the will of God that other three years should be spent battling with the scribes and Pharisees, the priests and the lawyers, the Jewish rulers and the Roman governors; setting forth the character of God, vindicating the claims of His law, and unfolding His own office and mission as Messiah; that during that time He should scatter all manner of blessings among the people, and perform those works of mercy which usually bring much credit to the worker, and raise his position in the world. But for all He did, His position remained as it was: He continued poor and homeless, the companion of fishermen, and often persecuted; yet always pleased, because it was the will of the Father.

It was the will of God that He should be subject to the ceremonial law; that He should be circumcised and baptized, though He needed no purification; that He should attend the Passover and other Hebrew festivals, though He needed no redemption. But no matter to Him how strange the requirements; it was enough for Him that it was His Father's will.

It was the will of God that He should be subject to the moral law in all its searching demands; that He should be meek under all manner of provocations, patient when goaded to excitement, kind and beneficent when treated with harshness and cruelty; that the stern command, "Thou shalt not steal," should frown on Him if, even on the earth which He created, He should stretch forth His hand to what was formally another's; and the not less stringent law, "Thou shalt not cover thy neighbour's house," if, not having where to lay His head, He should be tempted to look wistfully at another's home. But He knew that it became Him to fulfill all righteousness; and whatever sacrifice it might cost Him, the Father's will was sacred in His eyes.

And as He ever had regard to the Father's will in what He did, so also in what He suffered. The suffering involved in saving men was, beyond all example, terrible. To suffer the penalty of the broken law; to be bruised by the sword of God; to have the treatment of an outcast and a malefactor — truly, no sorrow was ever like His sorrow. Yet how beautifully all was borne! What a contrast between the spirit of the first Adam and the second in their respective gardens — the one in Eden, the other in Gethsemane. How lightly the one treats the divine will; how awfully it is regarded by the other. It was no wonder that the human nature relieved itself with the cry, "If it be possible, let this cup pass from me." But hardly was it uttered when that beautiful "nevertheless" was sent to recall it — "Not my will, but thine be done."

Hitherto we have simply stated certain obvious facts in our Lord's life and experience. His Father's will was alike the rule of His life and the delight of His heart. But how came it to be so? In what light did that will present itself to Jesus, so that while He obeyed it with such profound submission, He felt in so doing such intense delight?

1. In the first place He felt that, intrinsically, its claims were overwhelming. They were such as to admit of no rival, and no compromise. Perhaps we may find a faint image of this feeling in the sentiment that, two centuries ago, bound the Royalists of this country to honor and obey their king. In their eyes the majesty of the king was most sacred. The King of England was the Lord's anointed, and, as his person was profoundly sacred, so his every command and wish were to be treated with unfaltering deference. All the more was such deference to be paid to him, because there were rebels and miscreants in the country who not only refused him his honors, but had the unparalleled presumption to take arms against him. No doubt, loyalty carried to such a height was an idolatrous feeling. But the very fact of its being idolatrous when applied to man makes it the better illustration of what is due, and of what was rendered by Jesus, to God. In the bosom of Jesus there prevailed that most profound reverence for the majesty

of God, of which the Cavalier's reverence for his king was the idolatrous equivalent. And when God was the object of the feeling it could not be too profound. To the mind of Jesus the Divine claims were infinitely sacred; august beyond conception; never to be tampered with; all things vile and horrible were concentrated in the spirit that refused absolute submission to the will of God. And all the more would He feel this, because the world, in its wicked madness, was treating it with such contempt. For the evil treatment by others of what we prize only deepens our regard. When the wife of Brown of Priesthill caught in her arms the body of her martyred husband, the honor with which she regarded him was only increased by the brutal treatment of Claverhouse. Who can fathom the working of the like feeling in the human soul of Jesus; each insult offered by infatuated men to the will of His Father only deepening His reverence — "*I delight* to do thy will, O my God."

Perhaps we may find a better illustration of our point in more familiar scenes. We know something of the reverence with which a dutiful child respects the charge of a dying parent. Is it a daughter watching the last suffering of a beloved mother? In the intensity of her sympathy, what would she not do to procure for her mother one painless breath, or one hour of refreshing sleep! The end is evidently approaching, and with a great effort the mother signals her to attend. She has a dying request to make of her — can she refuse? Nay, all her life long that dying request is cherished in her heart; to fulfill it, no burden is deemed too heavy, no sacrifice is deemed too great. Now, to the soul of Jesus, every expression of the Father's will was as sacred as if it had been a parent's dying request. The very thought of disregarding it would have caused a thrill of horror — If I forget Thee, O my Father, let my right hand forget her cunning; let my tongue cleave to the roof of my mouth, if I prefer not Thy will above my chief joy.

2. But again, the Divine will was very dear to Jesus from its connection with the work and the reward of redemption. Subjection to the Divine will, in action and in suffering, was the condition of redemption — the condition on which Jesus was to bring His many sons to glory. The glory of the future was thus ever reflected on it. There was ever present to His mind the connection between what He had to do and suffer, and what His people were to reap. And thus the pain of the present was neutralized by the anticipated joy of the future. The will of God, in its greatest exactions, became not only endurable, but sweet. Shall I not drink of this cup, we may fancy Him saying, when millions of immortal beings

are to be brought to glory, honor, and immortality? when a dying thief is to be converted at my side? when a Saul of Tarsus is to become a holy missionary? when earth's wildernesses are to be turned into gardens? when heaven is to be peopled by myriads, once, many of them, fornicators and murderers and extortioners, but washed and sanctified and justified in my name and by my Spirit?

Let us mark here the bearing of an unselfish *end*, on an unselfish *rule* of life. The purpose for which Christ lived and died was unselfish — to bless others with eternal life; and the fondness with which He cherished this unselfish end exalted the unselfish rule. Living in the joy of the coming blessedness of His people, He could serenely and contentedly bow to that will by which their glory was secured.

3. Yet again; there was delight from the very fact that there could be no collision between the Father's will and His own. The perfect unity of will between them was a great source of joy. Let us consider the effect of collision, even between human wills. It is from such collision that nearly all our social miseries come. It is the source of wars and quarrels, of strifes and lawsuits, of

plots and counterplots, of assaults and robberies and crimes without number. And if the collision of one human will with another be so disastrous, far more disastrous is the collision of any creature's will with God's. Satan's will came into collision with God's; he was cast down, and confined in chains of darkness. Adam's will came into collision with God's; there followed the Fall, and its world of woes. Man's will is ever coming into collision with God's, but only to verify anew the woe — "Woe unto the man that striveth with his Maker!"

Unity of will is the necessary condition of social enjoyment, and especially of enjoyment between man and God. But how is it to be attained? If there be a natural antagonism, one of the two wills must subdue the other. Which must it be? God's or mine? The question may be started, but it were blasphemy to linger over it. Our blessed Lord has solved the problem. His human will, in all its deliberate and final actings, was absorbed by God's. And this, in itself, was peace. To say, I will give up all to God — my own pleasures, interest, profit, honor, comfort — I will have no will of my own about these things, God shall regulate them all — is peace indeed. "Oh, what a blessed thing it is," said the dying Payson, "to lose one's own will. Since I have lost my own will I have found happiness. There can be no such thing as disappointment for me, for I have no desires but that God's will may be accomplished."

What important lessons are here for all Christians, for the guidance of their inner life! Is it my business to do God's will, and is it my delight? Is it my *business*? Is it the rule I lay down for myself each morning? is it the standard by which I try myself at night? Has there been any collision of will during the day, or any threatening of a collision? and if so, which of the two has been subdued by the other? Has the thought pervaded my heart, as a silent but unquestioned force, that it were alike the height of madness and the depth of wickedness to set my will above the will of God? Have I been taught the "I must" of my Lord?

And is it my *delight* to do God's will? Do I know the joy of being one with Him? Do I know the happiness of conquering my lower nature, and entering into the freedom of a son — the glorious liberty of the sons of God? Do I bring the glory of the future to bear on the struggles of the present? Have I learned my Lord's "I will"?

Let it be granted that to these questions a perfect answer can be given by no living man; yet are they questions which it is absolutely necessary for us to deal with, and to deal with earnestly. Never let us turn the grace of God into lasciviousness. Never let us dazzle and deceive ourselves with one side of the truth, glorious though it be — that the grace of God comes over all the sins and deficiencies of man. If we have received this glorious grace, we must have been taught to aim at doing the will of God. And no man can be a Christian who is not trying to do that will, and to surrender his own. No man can have the spirit of Christ who does not know the feeling that what he has done has pleased God, and that this is far better than if it had pleased himself. And no man who is not thus trying day by day to please God can have any inheritance in that kingdom of which our Savior said, "Not every one that saith unto me, Lord, Lord, shall enter into the kingdom of heaven; but he that doeth the will of my Father which is in heaven."

HIS ENTIRE HARMONY WITH THE FATHER

"The Son can do nothing of himself, but what he seeth the Father do." — John 5.19

To the captious spirit of His enemies we owe one of the most remarkable assertions our Lord ever uttered of His oneness with the Father, and of the bearing which this had on the whole course of His human life.

It was at Jerusalem, on occasion of one of the feasts, and after the cure of the impotent man at Bethesda, that the occurrence took place. An accusation was brought against Jesus on the ground that the cure was performed on the Sabbath day. The accusation was a common one, ready, indeed, for use on many occasions; and Jesus had different ways of meeting it. One was a simple and ready method, the *argumentum ad hominem* — the appeal to what they themselves would do if their ass or their ox should fall into a pit on the Sabbath day. The other was a profounder method, derived from a Divine analogy — from what the Father did in the like circumstances; and it is of some interest to notice that this reply is recorded only by St. John, the most profound of the Evangelists. The accusation against Jesus was, that He had shown Himself at discord with the Father by working on the Sabbath. In His reply, He not only denied the charge of such discord, but affirmed the existence of a degree and kind of harmony between Himself and His Father, such as earth cannot match, and our faculties can hardly conceive. You think I would keep closer to my Father by not healing on the Sabbath day. I tell you that in what I have done I have been in the closest possible sympathy with my Father. There is not a thought in my heart, nor a movement of my hand, but is in precise agreement with Him. "My Father worketh hitherto and I work." "I and my Father are one."[1]

---

1   "But Jesus answered them, My Father worketh hitherto, and I work. Therefore the Jews sought the more to kill him, because he not only had broken the sabbath, but said also that God was his Father, making himself equal with God. Then answered Jesus, and said unto them. Verily, verily, I say unto you, the Son can do nothing of himself, but what he seeth the Father do: for what things soever he doeth, these also doeth the Son likewise. For the Father loveth the Son, and showeth him all things that himself doeth: and he will show him greater works than these, that ye may marvel. For as the Father raiseth up the dead, and quickeneth them; even so the Son quickeneth whom he will. For the Father judgeth no man, but hath committed all judgment unto the Son: that all men should honour the

Two views might be taken of the meaning ot His reply. On the one hand, it might be thought to teach that on the Sabbath day the Father, as the God of providence, worked in a way parallel to that in which Christ had worked. The Father does not stop the healing agencies of nature on that day. Tear a branch from a pine tree on the Sabbath; the wounded tree will immediately distil its resin over the gash, thus making a kind of plaster for the wound. Inflict a wound in like manner on the human body; the blood will by-and-by become clotted, and the beginnings of a new skin will be formed. The *vix naturæ medicatrix* — the power of God the Preserver — is as active on the Sabbath day as on any.

Son, even as they honour the Father. He that honoureth not the Son, honoureth not the Father which hath sent him. Verily, verily, I say unto you. He that heareth my word, and believeth on him that sent me, hath everlasting life, and shall not come into condemnation; but is passed from death unto life. Verily, verily, I say unto you. The hour is coming, and now is, when the dead shall hear the voice of the Son of God: and they that hear shall live. For as the Father hath life in himself; so hath he given to the Son to have life in himself; and hath given him authority to execute judgment also, because he is the Son of man. Marvel not at this: for the hour is coming, in the which all that are in the graves shall hear his voice, and shall come forth; they that have done good, unto the resurrection of life, and they that have done evil, unto the resurrection of damnation. I can of mine own self do nothing: as I hear, I judge, and my judgment is just, because I seek not mine own will, but the will of him that sent me." — John 5.17-30

Even if this had been all that Christ meant to say, it would have amply vindicated the healing of a helpless sufferer. His work was only of a piece with the Father's. He had used His extraordinary powers of healing just as the Father made use of the ordinary powers. In going alongside of His Father, in keeping step with Him, He had but acted like every faithful servant, like every dutiful son.

But it is clear that Christ's words went deeper than this. If this had been all their meaning the Jews would not have accused Him of calling God His Father in a peculiar sense (*patera idion*), thus making Himself equal with God (ver. 18). When we examine His words with care we find that they bear this fuller and deeper meaning — that, in healing that impotent man, Jesus had acted as the organ of God; He had not done it at His own hand, or at the impulse of His own will merely; He had done it by the will and agency of the Father, acting in this, as in similar matters, in and through His Son.

And this becomes to Christ a text for a wonderful sermon on the unity of soul and unity of operation — of inward state and outward act — characteristic of the Father and the Son. He brings out the truth on this subject in three chief propositions.

1. The Son can do nothing of Himself, but what He sees the Father do.

2. The Father shows the Son all that He is doing.

3. The Father makes the Son the medium or organ through whom He works; and that, too, not merely in matters comparatively trivial, like the healing of a lame man, but in matters of overwhelming magnitude: such as quickening men's souls, raising the dead, and judging the world — works which are pre-eminently works of God, but which are performed by the hands, and through the will, of the Son.

From these propositions our Lord draws the inference that the doing of these works of the Father by the Son is the true evidence of the Son's mission and claims. Where there is a spiritual eye to see this oneness of Jesus with the Father, no other evidence is needed of His Divine authority and standing. Whoever understands aught of God's purposes and operations, and sees these fulfilled and executed by Jesus, knows that Jesus is the Son of God. On the other hand, inability to see this connection, inability to see how Christ is the organ of the Father, and how the work of healing and quickening done by Christ is the fulfillment of the Father's plans and purposes, argues complete spiritual blindness. Such men are in a most hopeless condition; for if they can see nothing of God in the manifestation of Him by the Son, what better means can be devised for bringing them to know Him?

When our Lord opens up the relations between the Father and the Son, it is not easy to say whether it is the Divine or the human nature of the Son that is present to His thoughts. No doubt it was His purpose, in the first instance, to vindicate the act just performed in the presence of the Jews by Him who stood before them; and therefore we should say that the human nature of the Son must be meant. But in that wonderful personality of Christ the Godhead is never absent; and in this discourse He seems at times to speak also of the eternal relations which subsist between the two Divine Persons. So close, indeed, is the analogy between the relation of the Eternal Son to the Fountain of Godhead, and the relation of the Son of roan to the Father, that the language which sets forth the one is suited, with but little change, to convey the other. "It is difficult to say," says Dr. Liddon, "whether He is speaking as man of the honour of union with Deity, and of the graces that flowed from Deity, conferred upon His manhood; or whether, as the everlasting Son, He is describing those natural and eternal gifts which are inherent in His Godhead, and which He receives from the Father, the Fountain or Source of Deity — not as a matter of grace or favour, but in virtue of His eternal generation."[2]

1. The first of our Lord's statements is that the Son can do nothing of Himself, but what He seeth the Father do.

The impossibility referred to is evidently a moral impossibility. It is not that the Son dare not do anything of Himself through dread of the consequences; nor is it that physically His powers are so tied up that they can be put forth only in the same line as that in which the Father is working; but that the Son is so thoroughly one with the Father as to be incapable of differing from Him, or of working apart from Him. Even earthly relations furnish instances of a similar impossibility. A musician of fine ear, singing or playing an accompaniment to another, cannot but sing or play in harmony; cannot go

---

2 Bampton Lectures on the Divinity of Christ, p. 274.

off into another tune. A mathematician versed even in the elements of his science, inquiring what is the sum of the angles of any triangle, cannot differ from another mathematician in holding that they are together equal to two right angles. In the more exact sciences this unity of view is the rule, not the exception; in matters less exact, it is not so common. In matters of taste, men proverbially differ; yet we may find two or more men so constituted that any picture, building, or scene that is admired by one of them excites, quite independently, the admiration of the others. So, in their moral sense, there may be found a similar unity. There are consciences that keep pace with each other like barometers; that cannot but approve or condemn alike. But it must be owned that it is very rare to find men who are alike all round. The nearer our conception comes to a complete unity — a oneness of the whole nature, intellectual and moral — the more rarely is such a thing to be found. And still more rare is it to meet with cases where unity of nature is followed by unity of practice; and where those who have been like each other in their views have been equally like in life and character.

But in the case of the Father and the Son the unity was complete. It was a oneness of the whole nature, and a oneness of the life. It was impossible for the Son to like anything which the Father did not like, or to do anything which the Father did not do. The whole nature of the Son moved in unison with the nature of the Father. What a contrast to fallen humanity, where all is out of gear, and where the last thing men would think of, for regulating their actions, is to look at what the Father is doing ! In that direction most men can see nothing. The eye is so unused to such investigation that it cannot get God into its focus; arid if it looks upwards, a confused, blurred image is all that it can discover. But the eye of Jesus was accustomed to peer into heaven, and it readily saw what the Father was doing. And once the eye saw it, the whole soul moved in sympathy. It could not do otherwise; could not but go in with the Divine plan.

Beautiful picture of God and man in harmony — of man in his true relation to God! Beautiful fulfillment of those dreamy longings which vaguely draw even fallen man towards God, although his sins tend to drive him away! Glorious outcome of the Divine purpose of God to unite Himself anew with humanity in Christ, and pour into it the fulness of His own nature! Let there be, though on a far lower level, such unity as this between God and us, such quickness to perceive His mind, such readiness to go on with His work; not only shall we have no sense of emptiness and vanity in our life, but, reaching the true perfection of our being, our souls shall be filled as with marrow and fatness!

But it appears that the Son was not left unaided to find out the things which the Father was doing. When He was so single-hearted in His desire to do them, the Father showed Him the pattern; for the rule of the kingdom is, "To him that hath shall be given, and he shall have abundantly;" and wherever on the servant's part there is an eager desire to see, there on the Master's part is an equal readiness to show.

2. This is Christ's second statement. "The Father loveth the Son, and showeth him all things whatsoever Himself doeth."

The desire of the Son to see the pattern is met by the readiness of the Father to show it. This also shows the working, in its perfection, of a law of unity of which there are found faint traces among ourselves. Unity of heart, or sympathy, engenders confidence. Approval of a friend's character and aims, and desire to cooperate in the accomplishment of his plans, are commonly met by the confidential communication of those plans. The more like-minded men are — husband and wife, for example — the fewer are the secrets between them. This, it seems, is the faint reflection of a profound law, which finds its completest fulfillment in the confiding intercourse of God the Father with Jesus Christ, His Son. The completeness of this sympathy leads the Father to show His plans to the Son, and enables the Son readily to apprehend them. Sympathy has eyes of its own to read the mind of another, and ears of its own to catch his thoughts and feelings. It is sometimes like a new sense. It was so in the case of Jesus. Jesus knew beforehand, for example, that it was God's purpose to raise Lazarus from the dead. "*Father, I thank thee that thou heardest me, and I know that thou hearest me always;*" and throughout His whole career on earth He intuitively apprehended the Father's plans. Let us just remark, in passing, how much more terrible, after a life of such sympathetic action, must have been that strange disturbance of their relations which forced the cry, "My God, my God, why hast thou forsaken me?"

3. Our Lord advances to a third position. The Father makes the Son the organ through whom His greatest and most characteristic acts are performed. The Father acts by the Son — does so even now, and hereafter will do so in a way more conspicuous. Even now by the Son

He heals the lame; even now He quickens dead souls; but hereafter the Son will be the organ not only of quickening souls, but of raising bodies and judging the world. And yet, so wonderful is the relation, that even when so influenced by the Father, the Son acts as an independent Person; His will is not superseded: "The Son quickeneth *whom he will*;" but it is in such harmony with the Father's that it ever leads to the same results.

"I can of mine own self do nothing," He says; "as I hear, so I judge: and my judgment is just; because I seek not mine own will, but the will of the Father which hath sent me."

We find ourselves here in a region beyond our depth. At one moment He says, "I can of mine own self do nothing;" at another He affirms it to be the Divine will "that all men should honour the Son, even as they honour the Father." Amid the haze of the light which is inaccessible, one thing is plain: that the moral unity, the identity of will, the sympathy between the Father and the Son, is perfect; the Father's choice as to who are to be quickened is responded to precisely by the Son; the Son's judgment to be executed on the quick and the dead will be in precise accordance with the Father's will.

Even in His human nature, the will of Christ never deviates by a hair's-breadth from the will of the Father. And yet there is to Christ perfect freedom, and the sense of freedom; like a stream whose motion is controlled throughout by the great law of gravitation, yet whose every ripple and eddy and dimple shows the very soul of liberty.

Now, what our Lord wished in the first instance to bring out from all this, was, that this manifest unity between Him and the Father was the most convincing evidence, to those who had eyes to see, of His Divine mission and standing. The appeal to miracles was an appeal to a lower faculty; although Jesus did not scruple to make such appeal in the case of those who had no organ of vision to apprehend His oneness with the Father. It was this higher and more spiritual evidence that made such a profound impression on the Apostle John. "We beheld his glory, the glory as of the only begotten of the Father, full of grace and truth." And beholding this glory. He was changed into the same image. There came to be a remarkable moral unity between Jesus and John. John had an insight into Christ's character and work, in their profounder relations, such as no other of His followers enjoyed. He remembered the discourses in which our Lord spoke of these things, when no one else recorded them. They lay within the sphere brightened and made interesting by His own experience. His memory cherished them, as the memory always cherishes that to which its most delightful and sweetest enjoyments are due.

But besides the lesson which the unity between Jesus and His Father teaches us regarding His claims, it serves to bring into prominence a great law of God's kingdom, applicable to all His servants. For in proportion to the moral unity subsisting between God and them is the degree of spiritual power which is entrusted to them. In the case of Jesus the unity was perfect; and to Him therefore the Father gave the Spirit "not by measure." In the case of men, even the most spiritual, the harmony is incomplete; but in proportion to its degree is the measure of the Spirit. And hence our Lord's constant aim was to produce and promote this harmony. By making them one with Himself, He sought to make them one with God, and thus invest them with God's power. By bringing them into sympathy with a human brother. He sought to bring them into sympathy with a Divine Father. It was a lofty aim. They were to be in the world as He was in the world. As the Father sent Him, so He sent them. As the Son could do nothing of Himself but what things He saw the Father doing, so the disciples were to do nothing of themselves but what things were done by the Son. And acting thus, they would share His power. "Verily, verily, I say unto you, he that believeth on me, *the works that I do shall he do also*, and greater works than these shall he do, because I go unto my Father."

Still more remarkable are the words in which, in the same farewell discourse, Jesus denotes the possibilities of harmony between His disciples on the one hand, and Himself and His Father on the other, and the results of that harmony. "He that hath my commandments and keepeth them, he it is that loveth me; and he that loveth me shall be loved of my Father, and I will love him, and manifest myself unto him. . . If a man love me, he will keep my words, and my Father will love him, and we will come unto him, and make our abode with him." What a glorious atmosphere of *loving sympathy* it is that all the parties to this fellowship breathe! The disciple loves Christ, Christ loves the disciple; the Father, who loves Christ, likewise loves the disciple. The effect of this on the disciple is that he keeps Christ's words; the effect on the Father and the Son is, that they come unto him, and make their abode with him. Delightful training, both in its method and in its effects! In its method — for this consists in surrounding them with an atmosphere of love, and teaching them to breathe it; in its effects — for then Christ's words are dear to them, and His indwelling brings both strength and peace.

We mark too, here, how the casting out of all desire for self-glory coincides with the reception of the highest glory. When self is cast out, and the only ambition remaining in us is to be organs of Christ for manifesting His love and conveying His saving power, the glory of the Lord surrounds the soul. Would that every servant of Christ sought eagerly to live in loving sympathy with the Father and the Son, and thus become an organ in His hand for manifesting His grace and doing His work in the world!

Sympathy with Christ is the subtle force through which the Holy Spirit moves the world. Before it the walls of Jericho fall, though neither battering ram nor cannonball are driven against them; before it the mountains skip like rams, and the little hills like lambs; old things pass away, and all things become things new.

HIS TEMPTATION BY THE DEVIL

"Then was Jesus led up of the spirit into the wilderness
to be tempted of the devil." — Matthew 4.1

The temptation of Jesus in the wilderness, during the fast of forty days, culminating in the threefold attack of the devil, is one of the most unexpected events in the whole narrative of His life. Singular in itself, it appears still more strange, at least on the first blush, to have happened at the time when it did. The long preparatory thirty years at Nazareth had come to an end. The qualities of the human nature had reached their state of thorough ripeness. Jesus had been baptized of John, and had received his testimony. The Holy Ghost had descended on Him visibly, and a voice had proclaimed from the open heavens, "This is my beloved Son, in whom I am well pleased."

One would have thought that without further delay Jesus would have now begun His public work. But we are mistaken. The thirty years must have a parallel in the forty days. The Spirit that has descended on Him, and endued Him with measureless power, does not lead Him to the battlefield, but to the wilderness. He leads Him out, not to attack the enemy, but to sustain the enemy's attacks upon Him. There is in this something contrary to our expectations, and thereby attesting the reality, the unfictitious character of the narrative. What mythical theory could find a motive for so strange a passage in the life of Christ?

But let us look a little deeper, and see whether a clear and beautiful light may not be brought to shine upon the transaction. In dealing with it, we shall have to view our Lord's person on its human side; we shall have to regard Him as "learning obedience by the things which he suffered;" as made "in all things like unto his brethren, that he might be a merciful and faithful high priest in things pertaining to God."

When the Holy Ghost descended on Jesus at His baptism, and the voice from heaven proclaimed Him to be the Son of God, His position was doubtless very glorious; but in reference to the feelings and tendencies of a human being, it was not without its dangers. It was the crowning of a long process, the triumph of a life-long strain of soul; but for this very reason it was liable to be followed by relaxation or slackening, such as we often see in a young communicant after partaking of the Supper; or in an anxious inquirer after attaining to peace, or in an earnest student after an examination that has cost him months of incessant study. But besides this, Jesus was now invested with new and remarkable powers. The coming down of the Holy Ghost was the symbol of supernatural power, and Jesus obviously felt this. We know that before this time He had wrought no miracle — in spite of the foolish statements of the Apocryphal Gospels; and we know that after this the devil addressed Him as one conscious of miraculous power. The peculiarity of His situation was that He had received an open assurance of the favour of the Father, and had been consciously invested with supernatural might. And it was here that the elements of danger to human nature lay.

For it is simply a matter of history that few men have been able without peril to wield remarkable powers of any kind, suddenly acquired. Very commonly such men have been marks for the shafts of the tempter. They come to feel as if ordinary rules were not made *for them*; as if they were above ordinary restraints, and were a law to themselves. Take the case of Saul, king of Israel, so modest and self-restrained before he came to the throne, so wild and reckless after he became conscious of kingly power. Take the case of Luther, in his conflict with Zwingle; or, indeed, the case of any Church leader in the hour of almost unlimited power; or take the case of the leaders of the first French Revolution; or the case of Napoleon divorcing Josephine, to marry a princess of Austria. Such cases show, both in men sanctified and in men unsanctified, the perils of sudden and extraordinary power. And even an assurance of God's favor clearly conveyed is not without its danger. Men who are not hypocrites have been known to presume on the sense of their spiritual elevation to play loose with the moral law; some subtle feeling getting into their minds that that elevation placed them above the necessity of minding the rules and restraints that are binding on other men.

It seemed good to God, then, that before Jesus entered on His public work He should pass through an ordeal to show that, in His case, sudden power and the assurance of the Divine favor had brought no such consequences. He, too, became a mark for the shafts of the tempter.

He sustained the ordeal in the wilderness, at a distance from His friends, not only without all human prop and encouragement to resist temptation, but in all the bodily weakness arising from want of food. But though the Prince of this world came, he found nothing in Him. At every point Jesus was more than conqueror.

The temptations of the devil were all skilfully directed to try the question whether Jesus was so thoroughly one with the Father as He professed to be, and as it was necessary that He should be; whether His Father's business really was the one interest of His heart and the great business of His life; whether His delight in doing God's will was so strong that it could not be overcome by any intenser feeling; whether, under high pressure, some discord might not be revealed between Him and the Father.

The skill and subtlety of the temptation at that particular hour in Christ's life show the work of a master. At the time when Jesus has been invested with all supernatural power, and when He has been publicly declared the Plenipotentiary of heaven, it is to be tried whether or not He retains all the lowliness and submission of a servant. At the time when God has declared Him to be

His beloved Son, in whom He is well pleased, it is to be tried whether, on the strength of that sonship, He cannot be induced to make a needless draft on His Father's care. At the time when He has received a world to conquer by the slow influence of truth, it is to be tried whether He cannot be persuaded to accept an alliance with an alien power that will infinitely simplify the labor of the conquest. Can He be induced, in short, at any point, to take a line of His own? or is He loyal to the core to His Father's will, incapable of seeking His own, having no end in life apart from His Father's glory? Is it absolutely and immutably true that "the Son can do nothing of himself but what things he seeth the Father do?"

The devil had no hope of getting Jesus to rebel against His Father. It would have been preposterous to have any such expectation of One who, from the day when He was left behind in the temple, had been so thoroughly devoted to His Father's work and His Father's will. But might not some subtle feeling be worked upon, inconsistent with the spirit of entire submission? Might not some human tendency be roused up to take a different line? Experience shows that there are not a few such tendencies liable to show themselves in the case of men entrusted with great power, enjoying the assurance of God's favor, and sent forth on a great and tedious enterprise. Is there not a tendency to use their power, at least occasionally, for their personal advantage? or to presume on the Divine favor of which they are assured, to incur danger rashly and unwarrantably? or to shorten their labor and lessen their difficulties by accepting for their enterprise a species of aid unworthy of the work and dishonoring to the Master? Can any of these tendencies be excited in Jesus?

1. Can He be tempted to use His power for any unwarrantable act of self-indulgence? He is faint and hungry through long fasting, and the craving for food is intense. Though He has no food in His hands, He has ample power of producing it. He has power to turn the very stones into bread. Why should He not use that power? In some way or other this thought is introduced by the devil into Jesus' mind. Why should the Son of God suffer such inconvenience, nay, serious damage to His body, when the means of averting it are at hand? May He not, like David with the shewbread, resort to peculiar measures in a peculiar emergency? Granted that His miraculous power was not conferred on Him for His own use, may He not call it in for a moment to remove the difficulty which has come upon Him? It can do harm to

no one, but it will be of great service to Him; it will at once remove an intolerable inconvenience, and strengthen Him for His work. Is it not a lawful means of preserving life, and therefore an actual duty?

But Jesus intuitively apprehends that this course is not in accordance with the Father's will. The miraculous power which He has received is for a sign to the world, not a mere convenience to Himself; His miracles are to be symbols of men's deliverance from the thraldom of evil, not mere sources of ease or comfort to the worker. That He is enduring a keen bodily craving does not show that the Father is pointing to this as the proper means of removing it; the presumption is that the Father would have Him to bear the inconvenience to the end. Of what avail then would it be to Him merely to preserve life, with the approval of the Father either withdrawn or lessened? Life, in the highest sense, so depends on the Divine approval in everything, on conformity with the Divine will all round, on unqualified compliance with every word that proceeds out of the mouth of God, that, without these conditions, bread is bread no longer, because it cannot sustain the only life which is precious to a Son of God.

Few things could bring out more clearly the completeness of our blessed Lord's surrender of Himself to the Father's will. It is not only that in all ordinary circumstances He keeps under His body and brings its every organ into subjection — ruling Himself most strictly in all matters of meat and drink and sleep and bodily habits generally — but that even the lawful claims of the body are resisted, and that, too, under pressing circumstances. For, when the interests of God's cause are concerned, there are claims more urgent than those of hunger, there are interests more precious than even life.

In sweeping this temptation aside, our blessed Lord gave the cue to many noble men and women among His followers who have shown themselves regardless of bodily comfort under the sense of Christian duty. The missionary who has banished himself from home, to live among savages; the physician who has tasked his every energy and braved every risk amid the ravages of plague or fever; the pilot who has stood by his helm while the ship was on fire, and held the wheel, though the skin was cracking on his fingers; the motherly Christian neighbor who has stinted herself of the necessaries of life to care for some family in utter destitution; the over-toiled Christian worker who, under failing health and advancing disease, has still struggled at his work, feeling that where there were souls to be saved, the business was too urgent for health or even life to be thought of; have shown themselves true disciples of this great Teacher, and proved in every age the power of the truth, "Man shall not live by bread alone, but by every word that proceedeth out of the mouth of God."

2. Baffled here, the tempter tries another hook. He cannot tempt Jesus to any act of self-indulgence, but may he not tempt Him to an act of self-display? A man in favor with his sovereign likes to show it to the world. On public occasions he likes to wear his stars and other badges of honor; especially if he be treated contemptuously by his fellows, he has a satisfaction in showing how differently he is regarded in a far higher circle. In so doing he breaks no commandment, he commits no actual sin, but he shows in a quiet way how his mind turns in upon self; he is not single-minded in seeking the honor of his sovereign; he is concerned to have a share for himself. Might Jesus not be brought under the influence of this temptation? What if the crowd of worshippers in the courts of the temple were to see Him descending unhurt through the air from its highest pinnacle? Would not that give them a new sense of the honor in which they should hold Him, and gain for

Him an attention not to be otherwise secured? Is it not reasonable that He should let it be seen that He is the Son of God? the more especially when there is a Divine promise providing for His safety in these very circumstances: "He shall give his angels charge concerning thee: and in their hands they shall bear thee up, lest at any time thou dash thy foot against a stone."

It was a subtle temptation to put self in the center. It was a temptation to reverse the relation of Master and servant; it would be calling upon the Master to wait upon the servant, rather than the servant to wait upon the Master. It corresponded to a temptation to which public men and public speakers are especially liable: to display their abilities; to attract attention; to court applause; and to find their satisfaction in the admiration of their hearers rather than in the faithful performance of their work. Nay, more: it would be calling on God for help to enable Jesus to display Himself. Such a course could not but be regarded by Jesus as showing a discord with the Father, as decided, though not as flagrant, as if He had directly disobeyed His will. It was a proposal He never could entertain. He had come to this world as a servant, and He had deliberately resolved to make Himself of no reputation. Whatever ways of danger the Father should require Him to walk in, He would enter without doubt or fear, confident that in serving Him in the ways of His appointment He would enjoy all needed protection. But never of His own accord would He plunge into danger to let the world see how God protected Him. He would do His work quietly and steadily, avoiding all display, and neither seeking nor desiring the applause of men.

In this noble humility our Lord set the example to that pure-minded band of followers whose hearts have been so fixed on the quality of their service as to allow no thought for the applause of their fellows. Disregarding fame and shrinking from public notice, they have judged themselves at best unprofitable servants, who have done that which it was their duty to do. Content that others should bear the praise and the reward, they have meekly endured the toil, the privation, and the reproach. What mattered it that they should never be heard of, if only the interests of their Master were promoted? What mattered it that they should be counted the offscourings of the earth, if the seed of truth should be planted in some fresh soil; if rills of the water of life should go forth into the wilderness; if the Name which is above every name should spread its fragrance in regions hitherto unknown? Yet such men and women have never been rare among the servants of

Christ. Happy Master, that can look on such servants! Blessed servants, inheriting the spirit of such a Master!

3. But even yet the tempter has not exhausted his wiles. The hardest thing for Satan and his school is to believe in pure, patient, disinterested goodness. There remains another arrow in his quiver. He knows the greatness and the difficulty of the work which Jesus has undertaken; he knows that He has got the heathen for His inheritance, and the uttermost parts of the earth for His possession. Possibly he understands the method in which the dominion of this empire is to be gained: truth and love are the only weapons which this new Conqueror is to use. To be effectual, these weapons must be brought to bear on each individual heart; a siege must be laid to every soul. This process must be multiplied all over the world. Inch by inch the Messiah must push His conquests, encountering in each case the natural opposition of the heart, and from time to time the confederate forces of all His foes. What a tedious and dreary prospect! Centuries may pass without much visible progress. The toil, and the disappointment, and the suffering, involved in such a process, are endless. Might not the desired result be reached in a shorter way? If Satan should agree to give up the world to Jesus at once; if he should withdraw all opposition, and leave

the field clear for Him to take possession; would this not be infinitely better? To impress the mind of Jesus with his power he contrives to show Him all the kingdoms of the world and the glory of them in a moment of time. And he offers to make over to Him his whole power and interest in them on one small condition. Jesus must do obeisance to him as a sovereign transferring his rights; He must fall down and worship him. It is but the movement of a muscle, it is but the act of a moment. How magnificent the return for such a trifling act! The toil of centuries saved, the immediate possession of such an empire secured for the mere bending of a knee!

"Get thee behind me, Satan; for it is written. Thou shalt worship the Lord thy God, and him only shalt thou serve." The immediate possession of the whole world is not for a moment to be dreamed of at the cost of even one act of disloyalty to God. Jesus would encounter ten thousand battles, would spend centuries in pain and disappointment, rather than so much as breathe a thought out of keeping with the claims of the great Lord of all.

And here, also, our blessed Lord leads a noble band. Many a man engaged in Christian service has deliberately accepted poverty and conflict, when, by some apparently insignificant compromise, he might have gained a position of ease and honor. An act of obeisance to a rich but unworthy man might have secured important benefits and saved much hardship and trouble; but no true heart would stoop to such a mode of advancing the kingdom of God. The principles and interests of Christ's kingdom are too sacred for the arts of diplomacy. A Henry IV may surrender his faith for a crown, but he only shows thereby how unworthy he is of Jesus Christ. The true servants of their Master are those who, like the martyrs of all ages, have preferred the dungeon and the stake with a good conscience, to the highest posts, in this world when obtained through even the minutest sacrifice of truth and righteousness.

In all our Lord's replies to the devil we see the predominance in His mind of what was due to God. "Man shall not. live by bread alone, but by every word that proceedeth *out of the mouth of God*." "Thou shalt not tempt *the Lord thy God*." "Thou shalt worship *the Lord thy God*, and him only shalt thou serve." Though He be a son, He has become a servant, and He is constantly overshadowed by the sovereign claims of the King. And not only would He ever obey Him; but in every act and word, in every thought and feeling. He would ever be in closest sympathy, in thorough harmony, with the Lord His God.

Oh, that as He was, so might we be in the world!

HIS LIFE OF MINISTERING

"Even as the Son of man came not to be ministered unto, but to minister, and to give his life a ransom for many." — Matthew 20.28

The earthly work of our blessed Lord was a ministry to man as well as a service of God. He not only resigned His own will to the Father, that He might work the work of Him that sent Him, but the particular work on which He was sent was that of ministering, in every form of lowly and self-denying service, to the children of men. "A servant of servants" was truly His office; and the service was a most exacting one, absorbing all the energies of His life, and issuing in an awful death. To become the servant of God was much for one who "thought it not robbery to be equal with God;" but to become the servant of man was a far deeper act of humiliation; and deepest of all was the crowning act of that service — "to give his life a ransom for many."

But though such service was humbling in one sense, in another it was both honorable and glorious. And in our Lord's feeling, the glorious aspect quite covered and superseded the humbling. During all His life of condescension, He shows no sense of humiliation. He stoops so low as to wash His disciples' feet without seeming to feel that He is stooping at all. Not only is He upheld by the thought that His work is His Father's business, but also by a sense of its inherent dignity. This appears in His statement of the ruling principle of His life. If the disciples are disputing who shall be greatest, He has a higher aim, the aim of His own life, to set before them. If, like the Gentiles, they are trying who shall have most dominion over others. He has something loftier to substitute for that poor ambition. Let them learn to measure greatness, not by the number of persons who do service to them, but by the number to whom they do service. In this, as in other things, it is more blessed to give than to receive. It is a higher act to use what is yours for the good of others, than to use what is theirs for the sole benefit of yourself. The true nobility of life is to be ever helping and serving. This was the conspicuous feature of His own life: "Even as the Son of man came not to be ministered unto but to minister, and to give his life a ransom for many."

It was nothing short of a revolution which our Lord introduced when He sent forth into the world this great rule of life. It stands right against the notions on which men are ever apt to act. The selfish instinct is an awfully strong one. It seems so desirable a thing to have other people to bear our burdens, to supply our wants, to make life smooth and easy for us, and not to be troubled with doing the like for them. It is so tiresome to be involved in other people's troubles, to be worried with their difficulties, and even to suffer for their sins and their follies. To enjoy the rank and the wealth that raise you above the toils and struggles of the multitude, devolving on others all that is in any way burdensome, is the height of felicity according to a common view. To occupy this position for a little at the end of life is counted worth all the sweat and struggle of its earlier years. The thing sought is not to obtain the service of others in lower things in order that you may be free to serve your generation in higher things — for that were quite a Christian aim; but it is to have others serving you in all possible ways, simply that you may be free to enjoy all the pleasures of life. Thus man makes himself the center of his little system. Like the sea anemone, he twirls his arms, making eddies all round him, to bring tribute to his feet. He arranges and adjusts the labor of his fellows to contribute to the same result. And the more abundant his eddies, and the more numerous the persons that work for his pleasure, and the greater the tribute that is borne to his hand, the higher commonly is his place of honor in the world, and the more undoubtedly is he counted a great and successful man.

But all these judgments of the world Jesus simply reverses and annuls. It is the servant of all that is greatest of all. The truly successful man is not he that has gathered most to himself, but he that has done most for others. Real wealth is not measured by the amount of one's property, but by the capacity to use it well. Greatness does not lie in ability to draw everything to one's self, but in ability to use what one gets for the good of the many. To live for God, and for God's sake to become the servant of others; to soothe the sorrows and lighten the burdens of the oppressed; to make the world's crooked places straight and its rough places plain; to rescue the perishing, raise the fallen, and cheer the desolate; to do all these offices of love with unwearying patience and self-denial, and not grudge the expenditure of ease and health and life itself, when called for; such is our Lord's idea of greatness; such was the life led by Himself; and such is the lesson which alike by example and by precept He has left for us all.

It is indeed the lesson of Christ's life from beginning to end. It is one of the chief lessons of His miracles, as it is also the burden of some of His most beautiful discourses; and even the lesser incidents of His life present the same feature, the same affectionate and considerate regard to the wants and feelings of all about Him.

Let us begin with the beginning of miracles — the marriage feast of Cana. It is not easy to make that miracle fall into rank with most of the miracles. It is not, like them, a symbol of redemption. But it bears on its surface this feature of our Lord's character — the spirit of ministering. It shows Jesus ministering, not indeed to the highest wants, but to the wants of the body, and to a class of these that do not involve necessaries, but only luxuries. The feeding of the multitude in the wilderness and the miraculous draught of fish, are miracles of the same order.

In His miracles of healing, we see Him ministering to another and very pitiable class of bodily wants. His discourses are ministries to the higher part of our nature — the intellect and the soul. At the gate of Nain, and in the cemetery of Bethany, we find Him ministering in a very touching way to the heart broken by sorrow. What, we may ask, constitutes the charm of the parable of the good Samaritan, but that it pictures the ministering spirit warmly at work, in spite of all sectarian chills? And in that chapter of our Lord's life which is by far the most wonderful — the story of the last days— one of the chief wonders is, the activity of the spirit that ministered to others, even at the climax of His own sufferings. He ministers to the disciples by washing their feet, by comforting them and praying for them and making them bright promises of future blessings; He ministers to the dying thief by an assurance so precious that heaven itself could have supplied nothing higher; He ministers to His mother by providing for her a son and a home. And yet this was but the by-play of that spirit of ministering which even then was at work in a far deeper and darker region. For in that hour He was bearing for His people the awful burden of their guilt; He was ministering to them redemption and salvation and life eternal. While no human being was ministering to Him, while the cry, "I thirst," met with no response save the mocking offer of the vinegar; while there was no loving heart to soothe Him with gentle acts or tender words in the struggle and agony of death. His heart overflowed with thoughts for the good of others, and every power of action and of suffering was strained to achieve their salvation.

Does not this constitute the great charm of Christ's life? It is not a lesser or incidental feature of it, but its great glory. The most critical eye can trace nowhere the cropping up of the selfish spirit. The vast power that Jesus possesses He never uses for personal ends. How little He cared for money appears from His committing the care of it to the least trustworthy of the apostles, and from His having to borrow a penny when He had occasion to refer to that coin. He is above minding worldly honor, and He is indifferent to the pleasures and luxuries of earth. Such things may be around Him and beside Him, but they have no interest for Him; His enjoyment lies in quite a different sphere; His passion is all to do good. The world He lives in is in disorder; His passion is to rectify its disorders. Men are wretched; He longs to see them happy. They are lying under a load of guilt; He pants to remove the load. They know not God as the God of love; He longs to reveal Him. And towards these gracious ends His whole soul unceasingly moves.

But there is this to be remarked in the ministering spirit

of Christ; that it is not a fruit of mere soft-heartedness, not a rush to stop misery anyhow, regardless alike of its origin and its bearing on other things. On the contrary, all Christ's life of mercy is regulated by the fact that it is man's sin that has brought His suffering, and that by his sin he dishonors God as well as injures himself. And while He never fails to remove any suffering that comes in His way, He lays all His stress on removing the sin that causes the suffering, and thus glorifying God as well as benefiting men. To accomplish this He places Himself in their room; He gives Himself as a sacrifice for them. He keeps nothing back; gives up everything for them. His spirit of ministering is equal even to this unprecedented sacrifice. Well may we say, as we survey His life, "Thou art fairer than the children of men."

Perhaps it may be said that if Jesus preferred that life, if He found His pleasure in it, and found no pleasure in a common, selfish life, then it was no praise to Him to follow it. No other kind of life would have made Him happy: what then was remarkable in His making choice of it? But who does not see that on this ground the highest actions ever performed would be stripped of all praise, however difficult and trying the conditions under which they were done? No doubt, "honesty is the best policy;" but is no praise to be given to him who has flung from him a thousand chances of dishonest gain? The martyr who lays his head on the block is happier in that act than he could have been if, a traitor to his convictions, he had saved his neck at the expense of his conscience; but is no honor for that reason to be given to the martyr? The higher and purer one's life, the greater is the inward felicity which it brings; but is a man to be thought little of who rejects all the outward advantages that dazzle and fascinate the common eye? The truth is, that when men give themselves in a true spirit to a high or ministering life, they are not influenced by the thought of advantage or enjoyment. They do not sit down, as a merchant would, to balance one thing against another, and conclude that on the whole the most desirable course is to live for others, not for themselves. The selfish spirit never reaches such a conclusion, and goes to work in no such way. That spirit knows only of present, material, worldly good, and seeks only the indulgence of the lower part of its nature. The unselfish spirit disdains to live for such things, however much it might enjoy them, and puts them deliberately away. It determines to live for higher objects, apart altogether from the question of happiness. To the eye of sense, in this higher life there is little to be found but toil and trouble and sacrifice. To choose it is to renounce the lower part of your nature; it is to stop your ears against the siren voices that come from the world; it is to vow a solemn vow to love higher objects than self-gratification in any form. But then it is, when the lower part of the nature is thus overcome, that the fountains of a higher enjoyment are opened. In turning deliberately from what fascinates sense you come upon the joys and glories of faith. In turning your back on the broken cisterns you come upon the fountain of living waters. You find that God has His own high refreshments and enjoyments for all who forsake father and mother and lands and houses for His sake. And though it was not for these that you made your choice, you find that the life which you have chosen is richer and happier than that which you foreswore. God has put gladness in your heart, more than in the time that their corn and their wine increased.

The human nature of Jesus, sinless though it was, was no doubt capable of feeling the attraction of many of the enjoyments of sense. And Jesus never frowns upon these as if He thought it wicked to gratify them. He does not, like St. Francis of Assisi, wed poverty as his bride, as if riches were wicked and poverty holy; but His eye is fixed on higher objects, and to get at these all the joys of sense are flung aside. The man does not despise clothing who flings his coat on the ground and plunges into the water to rescue a drowning fellow-creature. When a world, so full of sin and misery, was appealing on every side for pity and help, Jesus gave Himself to redeem it. He flung from Him whatever might hinder His noble work. Higher and more urgent than any other work seemed that of ministering to this doomed and stricken world; but the more difficult the task, the more was He stimulated towards it. His whole soul went out in His ministry. Never should it be said of Him that a chance was ever given Him of ministering to any of His brethren of which He did not eagerly avail Himself. Never should it be said of Him that any robbed and wounded traveler lay by the way and that He passed by on the other side. Nay, if the case of men demanded a higher mode of ministering; if lives forfeited by transgression demanded that another life should be offered in their room; if the awful chastisement of sin must be borne by another before they could be blessed; even that service was not too much for Jesus, His life was ready for the offering. "Sacrifice and offering thou wouldest not, but a body hast thou prepared for me. . . . Then said I, Lo, I come to do thy will, O God."

All through His life, therefore, the soul of Jesus was full of the interests of others, bodily, spiritual, and eternal. As the work of their redemption infinitely surpassed all other interests, both in its importance and in the difficulty which it involved, it could not but hold the chief place in His thoughts. But, terrible though this burden was, it did not prevent Jesus from undertaking other burdens, and keeping His eyes and His heart open for any disorder that He could remedy, or any trouble that He could soothe. That gentle look, those tender tones, that gracious and courteous manner, were all molded by the spirit of ministering; they were fruits of that love which, shrinking from everything that could increase disorder, sought on every side to make the crooked straight and the rough places plain.

If this spirit was so conspicuous in the Master, it must surely be a prominent feature in every consistent disciple. It constitutes, indeed, the great family likeness in every age and clime. If any man have not this spirit of Christ's, he is none of His. Yet how many are there, even in the high places of the Church, who are lamentably deficient in it! They may be very zealous, very regular, very orthodox, amazingly diligent in upholding their Church, shocked at false doctrine and irregular practice; but they are bitter, intolerant, unloving, and even malignant. In vain you listen for the soft answer that turneth away wrath; in vain you look for the sympathetic spirit that considers the case of others, or the charity that suffers long and is kind. Hard to their servants, exacting to all their dependents, nursing hatred, and cherishing the memory of wrongs, they are as bad as the disciples who would have called down fire from heaven to consume the Samaritan village. Well for them if they hear the Master's rebuke in this life; they run such a risk of hearing in awful tones on a future day — "I never knew you: depart from me, ye that work iniquity."

On the other hand, we sometimes find both men and women deficient in many ways, but rich in the spirit of ministering. We find them, perhaps, in Churches of which we do not think well, or in connection with a creed which we abhor. Let us not for such reasons think little of their spirit, but rather magnify the grace of Him who makes the flower bloom in the desert, and the birch and pine tree spring from a cleft of the naked rock. And for ourselves, surely, the right lesson must be, If the desert or the rock can show such fruitful plants, how much richer fruit should be found on those in reference to whom God asks, "What could have been done more to my vineyard, that I have not done in it?"

It is our happiness in these times to witness not a few new developments of the spirit of ministering, in men and women giving up a life of self-indulgence on behalf of the heathen abroad, or the miserable at home. All honor to their noble choice! Rich be ever their enjoyment of that pure joy which comes from every act of genuine mercy! And if at times the sense of hardship comes over them, and the wish arises to drink again the waters of some well of Bethlehem, as in the days of their youth may a deeper feeling swiftly follow: how much higher than any pleasure of sense is the joy of recovering a lost sheep on the mountains, and, like the good Shepherd Himself, bearing it rejoicing to heaven!

And how blessed is it, that in the very act of accepting Christ's ministry for us, we get the spirit of ministering for Him, Have you no desire to serve in this ministry? Is it irksome, repulsive, toilsome? Surely you cannot have accepted Christ's ministry for you. Have you not refused to accept of Him *as your ransom*? You do not feel that you need a life to be given as a ransom for you; and so there is no sympathy between you. But let the truth be realized that Christ's life was given for your life; that Christ died in your room, and to save you from dying; how different will your feeling be! What a powerful force, what a profound sympathy with His ministering love will now be kindled in your heart! It is this force that moves the world; that summons men and women from the bowers of worldly ease to the standard of Jesus, and sends them forth to the snows of Siberia and the fever swamps of Africa, willing, hearty, happy laborers in His cause.

It may not be the will of God that many should leave the sphere where Christ has found them. But what a blessing is the ministering spirit in every sphere! What a blessing to find it in the young: to find them resolving, while life is yet before them, that self-indulgence shall not tempt them to increase the disorder of the world; but that it shall be the ambition of their lives to leave it in some way better and brighter than they found it! Happy they who, as the shades of evening fall around them, can think that they have tried, however imperfectly, to follow their Lord in His spirit of ministering. True, indeed, even at the eleventh hour, if one is oppressed by the conviction that, instead of having lived like Christ to benefit mankind, one's life has been spent in increasing the evil and disorder that abound, it is not too late to obtain forgiveness. But how much better, both then and always, to have spent one's life in the Master's shadow, in the Master's footsteps; preaching good tidings to the poor, binding up the broken-hearted, and leaving hues of paradise on some dark spot of the desert!

HIS SYMPATHY WITH MAN

"In all their affliction he was afflicted." — Isaiah 63.9

No feature of our Lord's earthly career is more conspicuous, or more likely to arrest every reader of His life, than the tenderness of His feeling for the woes and sufferings of men. It is evident at a glance that He was profoundly impressed by the sorrow-stricken aspect of human life. It did not come before Him merely as a passing reflection; it was a matter of deep, frequent, almost constant contemplation. It did not present itself as something too painful to be studied, or too vast to be remedied. Painful though it was, it filled His soul, and its vastness only roused effort and sacrifice to provide a remedy. Were there nothing else to prove Christ more than man, His attitude in the face of the world's misery would surely be enough. Exquisitely acute in His sensibilities. He can yet survey and take in the whole sorrow and suffering of humanity. Profoundly impressed with the depth of the disease and the magnitude of the disorder. He yet undertakes to find a remedy. If only Jerusalem were willing. He could save her from ruin as effectually as a hen that gathers her chickens under her wings. If only the weary and heavy laden would come to Him, He would give them rest.

It is singular what differences there are in the feelings with which men commonly regard the sorrows and sufferings of their kind. Some, utterly regardless, spread misery around them in its most horrible forms and in endless profusion; like the conqueror to whom hecatombs of slain men are but ordinary incidents of war; or the slave-stealer, to whom the extremest anguish is nothing if there be but a chance of gain; or the libertine who, for the base pleasure of an hour, consigns a heart to misery and a life to ruin. Then we come to those who will not consciously produce such misery, but who look on it unmoved when it comes under their view. The priest and the Levite would not have assaulted the poor traveler, but when they see him in his extremity they pass by on the other side. Next, we find some who cannot see sorrow nor hear of it without pity, and possibly without some endeavor to mitigate it. It is a painful sight, and, like other painful sights, they would fain have it removed. But let others deal with it, not them; let others touch the offensive thing; they will give their money to help, but they will not let the smooth and easy course of their life be disturbed by personal dealings with misery and woe.

But there is yet another and a higher class. Some devote themselves to search out misery and relieve it. The cry of woe, so repulsive to others, is in a sense an attraction to them. Wherever there is distress, they take it home to their hearts; they make it their own; they live to lessen it. They identify themselves with the sufferers, they are ever thinking of them, they cannot rest till they are relieved. It is not merely that the relief of suffering appears to them one of the noblest purposes of life, but that they are impelled towards it by the strongest inward forces; so that it would be a moral impossibility for them to plunge into the stream of personal indulgence and forget the miseries of their brethren.

Need we say whose image and superscription it is that this last class bear? Who is the head and leader of this sympathetic company, this company of brothers and sisters "born for adversity"? The most intense and ardent of the band has but a tinge of the spirit of which the very essence and fulness belong to Christ. When we think of our Lord's outward life, it is the career of One who went about "healing all manner of sickness and all manner of disease among the people." When we penetrate to the deeper principles that impelled Him, we find that what affected him most was man's alienation from God and God's alienation from, man; and that He gave His very life, the just for the unjust, to heal the breach and restore the severed fellowship. The misery of His people was to Him no mere unpleasant sight, obtruding itself occasionally upon His notice, from which He was fain to turn His eyes whenever He could: it was something that He took up into His very heart; He made it His own; He could not forget it; He could not leave it alone. His heart could not rest while this misery continued. The pang of His suffering brethren went through Him as if it had been His own. He could no more cease to think of it than a man writhing in bodily torture can forget his agony, or act as if nothing were wrong.

There is all the difference in the world between these two ways of regarding another's suffering. On the one hand, placing it outside yourself — pitying it, no doubt, but still giving it a wide berth, as if you would rather anything than that it should come near to you; and, on the other hand, taking it inside your own heart, bearing the burden of it, and exerting yourself to mitigate it or remove it, as if it were your own personal sorrow. How priceless are friends of this order to those who are in trouble, how quickly they are recognized, how intensely they are loved! How strange it often seems to those who are merely kind, though very kind, that, while they can earn only thanks, the others secure warmest and purest love! It is not a matter to be reasoned about, for it is simply one of our intuitive judgments, that this sympathy which identifies itself with another's suffering is the most golden quality of the human heart. How glorious to find it so conspicuous in the character of our Lord — to find alike in the Old Testament and the New so prominent allusion to the tenderness of His fellow-feeling! "In all their affliction he was afflicted." "We have not an high priest which cannot be touched with the feeling of our infirmities; but was in all points tempted like as we are, yet without sin."

But while our Lord's sympathy was very tender and very true, it was not one-sided. Human sympathy often is so. It tempts one to be partial to its objects; to defend them and comfort them even where they may be greatly to blame. Sympathy is thus liable to become loose and soft, and to overlook the higher demands of truth and righteousness. Now, to estimate aright our Lord's sympathy with man, we must take into account His regard for His Father, and inviolable reverence for His will. As our previous chapters have shown, our Lord was in closest fellowship with the Father, interested profoundly in all His plans; He had devoted Himself without reserve to do His work and obey His will. It was impossible, therefore, that His sympathy with man, however intense, should make Him either do or desire anything in man's interest that was not in harmony with the will and glory of God. It could never induce Him to take man's side, as it were, against God, or to desire for man indulgence or connivance for transgressions, great or small. It could never lead Him to do, as a fond but weak mother sometimes does, take the part of the children against the father, and wink at their violation of his rules. Our Lord could never fall from that boundless reverence for the Divine will, as the high and indefeasible rule for all God's creatures, which lay, as we have seen, at the very root of His human nature. However keenly He might feel for the sufferings of men. He could not but feel still more vehemently that the Divine order must be upheld, the will of God must be honored. God, the Alpha and the Omega, the first and the last, of whom and by whom and for whom are all things: never could one act be done or one thought cherished by our blessed Lord, inconsistent with His sovereignty, or casting the faintest shadow on His inviolable majesty.

The human sympathy of Christ thus appears a very different thing from that supreme regard for man so often met with in modern literature, commonly called humanitarianism. According to this system, man is the true center of the universe. Man takes the place of Joseph's star and of Joseph's sheaf — the other stars and the other sheaves bow around him. The promotion of man's welfare is the highest object. Man has his failings and weaknesses; he has his faults, not to say vices; but it would be a cruel law that bent itself against these; it would be a terrible government that visited them with severity. The government of the world must adapt itself to man as he is. He must not be hemmed in and pinned down at every point; he must have freedom, his inclinations must be respected, his eccentricities must be pardoned. The moral order of the world must be relaxed for him; where his interests require it, other considerations must go to the wall. One needs to pause and think how terrible and how perilous is this man-exalting spirit which works with such subtlety in much of our literature. Under the guise of a profound and thorough sympathy with man, it causes him to change places with God. God becomes the servant of man, not man the servant of God. The song of the angels is transposed, and the purpose of the gospel comes to be, "Glory to man in the highest; on earth, peace; goodwill to God."

In the view of a sympathy which has thus gone so far astray, it is reassuring to turn to the case of Jesus, and to find that there is yet ground for a holy sympathy with man — a sympathy that enters at once both into his sins and sorrows, and seeks to remove them; while at the same time it has profound regard to the will and the honor of God. We know from the whole tenor of revelation how thoroughly, in all His sympathy with man, our blessed Lord was actuated by regard for the claims of God's law. The removal of man's misery could not be an act of simple clemency on the part of God; it could be accomplished only through an atonement that should amply satisfy His justice. The happiness of man could not be effected by relaxing the law to meet his feeble nature; atonement must be made by Jesus Himself for all man's transgressions, and his nature must be renewed and strengthened to respect God's will as the great rule of his being.

It is in these holy lines that the sympathy of Jesus ever runs. If men would be blessed, they must come to Him.

They have still to deal with the Father, and the Father still has regard to that law which is holy and just and good. Men have still to stand in the light of that word which is quick and powerful, and sharper than any two-edged sword, piercing even to the dividing asunder of the soul and spirit, and of the joints and marrow, and is a discerner of the thoughts and intents of the heart. The sympathy of Jesus procures nothing like indulgence or connivance. But it procures forgiveness full and free, and acceptance cordial and entire; it procures the Father's kiss and welcome, and the songs of angels over the son who was dead and is alive again, who was lost and is found. It procures these things in the light of day, and in the face of an immutable moral law; because it rests on that work of propitiation in which the Father "made him to be sin for us, who knew no sin; that we might be made the righteousness of God in him."

Having said so much of the holy conditions of our Lord's sympathy, we now turn back to the thing itself. We have said that His spirit was eminently marked by the highest quality of sympathy — by His making the case of others His own, and feeling and acting as if He were personally affected by their troubles. We find this quality both exemplified in His actions and reflected in His teaching.

Let us look, first, at His actions. Perhaps in every case of suffering relieved by Him we may find some indication of His taking it home to Himself, allowing it to come into His very heart. But this is more apparent in the case of His more intimate friends, and most apparent of all in His dealings with those who were so dear to Him — the family of Bethany.

It is a very strange incident in the story of Lazarus — the delay of Jesus in going to the stricken house. That looked the very opposite of sympathizing; as if Jesus wished to put this sorrow far from Him; did not wish His heart to be lacerated by it; shrunk from the pain which could not but spring from close contact with such grief. It may have looked like that, but it was the opposite of that. No sympathy could have been more profound than that which He showed with the afflicted sisters. We see how He entered into their case, by His whole demeanor beside them; by His signs of distress; by His groans and His tears. In one sense it is very strange that He should have been so much moved. Before He set out for Bethany He told His disciples that he went to awake Lazarus out of his sleep. When He entered the cemetery He knew that before sunset that evening Lazarus would be with his family, alive and well. We might have thought that the near prospect of so happy an event would have swallowed up our Lord's distress. And so doubtless it would, had he felt for Himself alone.

It was His intensely sympathetic nature that made it otherwise. He took the grief of these sisters — their present grief, the grief of that particular hour — home to His heart. He made it His own. He groaned and wept, under the influence of His sympathy.

Oh, there is a world of instruction and encouragement here! If Jesus had not felt the grief of Mary and Martha, if He had not felt it during that hour, if all sense of their pain had been swallowed up in Him by knowledge of their coming joy. He could not have felt the grief of any of us in this world. For we know that all the grief of believers is momentary grief; our light affliction is but for a moment; compared with the eternal joy, the weeping endures only for a night. But then we do not feel this. The night sometimes seems as if it would never drag through; the little season of Christ's absence seems anything but little. "Domine," exclaims St. Bernard, "tuum aliquantulum est longum aliquantulum." How blessed to know that, short though our grief is, and even though the streaks of dawn may be already in the sky, our Lord makes it His own. He measures it with our measure; He scans it from our point of view. Like a parent who seems actually to feel the hunger of his little child, though he knows that in one short hour it will all be gone, so Jesus seems to feel our troubles, though He knows that in a little while they are to end for ever. Wonderful grace! He both provides eternal glory for us at the close of life's little journey, and taking our troubles up into His own heart while they last, lightens the burden and cheers our spirits as we go up through the wilderness!

Next let us glance at our Lord's teaching as illustrating His sympathy. In what way does He teach His people to deal with other men's troubles, when their thoughts or their eyes are directed to them?

Let us turn for the answer to two of His parables — the Good Samaritan, and the Sheep and the Goats. What method of dealing with the wounded traveler does He commend in the good Samaritan? The priest and the Levite who passed by on the other side are only introduced as a dark background to the picture. The man who is so much commended is a man of genuine sympathy; he does not shrink from close contact with misery. He goes up to the wounded traveler, binds up his wounds, pouring in oil and wine: then he sets him on his own beast, and brings him to an inn, and takes care of him. And on the morrow, when he must depart, he takes out twopence and gives them to the host, and says to him, "Take care of him: and whatsoever thou spendest more, when I come again, I will repay thee." What a genuine interest, what a pure sympathy is here! The Samaritan feels for the troubles of the traveler as if they were his own, and is as eager to have them removed as if they were pressing upon himself. And have we not in this just the reflection of the Lord's own sympathy and treatment of His people, taking up their burdens and sorrows as His own, and unable to rest till they are all removed?

The other parable is that of the Sheep and the Goats. It illustrates the sympathy of Christ in a different aspect; how for a different purpose He identifies Himself with the sufferings and sorrows of His people; not directly to remove them, but to enhance the value both of the act and the reward to all who, for His sake, take trouble in connection with them. Jesus and His people are one; and all acts done in His name are regarded as done to Himself. If the contact between Christ and His afflicted people be such, how well He knows them, how much He thinks of them!

When Scripture invites us to follow Christ into heaven, it encourages us to think especially of His sympathy. His intercession before the throne is the fruit of it. As our High Priest, He is emphatically marked by this quality. His possession of human nature and His experience of human life have qualified Him for this function of priesthood. "In all things it behoved him to be made like unto his brethren, that he might be a merciful and faithful high priest in things pertaining unto God, to make reconciliation for the sins of his people. For in that he . . . suffered being tempted, he is able to succour them that are tempted."

What is here said as to His own life indicates the experience that has made sympathy possible for Him and helped Him to attain it. He could have had no such fellow-feeling had His life not been like our life, and His temptations like our temptations. We can easily understand, for example, how Christ should have an especial sympathy with persons who meet their death by the process of crucifixion. He knows so well its pains and its temptations. But in some degree He has a fellow-feeling also with every human being whose lot is to traverse the sea of life and encounter its stormy billows. He knows all the difficulties of the navigation, for He had to steer His own vessel through those rocky channels. He knows how strong are the attractions that drag men down when they are trying to rise upward. This makes it easier for Him to identify Himself with men, to take up their troubles and their burdens, and to transact for them before the throne. It gives emphasis to His asking for them mercy to pardon and grace to help. For whatever Jesus may know of the force of temptation, He never pleads for indulgence to any man; never asks that his sins may be passed over in silence, or not reckoned as faults. No act of His can ever lead men to think lightly of sin. The tendency of all His dealings is the very opposite — to reveal more clearly its hateful features, as the abominable thing that God hates. What He seeks for us is a far more thorough separation from sin than any indulgence could effect; the entire removal of its guilt through the merit of His own propitiation, and the destruction of its power through the renewing grace of His Holy Spirit.

It is strange that it should ever have been thought that the sympathy of Jesus is not tender enough, and that it is desirable to have it supplemented by that of Mary. Must not this perversion of the truth have arisen from great ignorance of what the sympathy of Jesus really means? If it be true that He takes the whole case of His people to His heart, and that He feels their troubles as if they were His own, does this leave anything further to be desired?

Besides, is not the notion that the sympathy of Jesus can be surpassed by that of Mary a reflection on the perfection of Christ's human nature? Let us grant that in ordinary life we commonly find a distinction between the sexes in the qualities in which they excel; let it be granted that, for the most part, women are more remarkable for gentleness, compassion, tenderness of heart and the more passive graces generally, while men are more gifted with courage, force, application, perseverance, and the like: yet if we conceive one in whom human nature is perfect, it is plain that he must be gifted with both classes of graces in their highest degree — those which are most conspicuous in the woman, as well as those which are most characteristic of the man. The compassion, the tenderness of Christ's heart, must have been perfect; not only not surpassed by another, but not even approached; and if in Him this tenderness was associated with the more manly graces, that union would only keep it from following a weak and hurtful course, would keep its current strong and healthy, in full accord with the will of God.

And now who can estimate the grandeur of the privilege of being in the fullest sense the object of this sympathy of our Lord? How blessed to think, in regard to any of us, that He takes us up into His heart just as we are, and that He cannot rest till all our sorrows and troubles, all our disorders and perversities, are brought to an end! What security does not this give us that our blessed Redeemer will persevere in the work which He has taken in hand! What confidence that He who hath begun a good work in us will carry it right to the end! His love is not a thing of fits and starts; His kindness is not a whimsical or fantastic attribute that turns with butterfly rapidity from one object to another. Having once loved His own that are with Him in the world, He loves them to the end; having once taken them into His heart and identified Himself with them, He cannot renounce them any more than He can renounce Himself; He can no more cease to feel their troubles than if they were His own. He has charged Himself with them, and He cannot disown the charge; he has agreed to conduct them to their Father's house; and at the end of His undertaking He is to say to the Father, "Those that thou gavest me I have kept, and none of them is lost, but the son of perdition; that the scripture might be fulfilled."

Perhaps it will be said that the view which we have given

of our Lord's sympathy proves too much. If He takes all who labor and are heavy laden into such close relation to Himself, it follows that in the end He must bring all of them to glory; if He cannot rest till one is safe, He cannot rest till all are safe. But this is not true. Many perish, even after Christ has had some dealings with them. The great end is not secured, even in some cases where a beginning seemed to be made. We are thrown here on that great mystery, that some "have been given to Christ by the Father, and that it is they only with whom Christ becomes so identified as to secure their final glory. "Thou hast given him power over all flesh, that he should give eternal life to *as many as thou hast given him*." "*Those that thou gavest me*, I have kept." "My Father, *which gave them me*, is greater than all; and no man is able to pluck them out of my Father's hand." Are these hard sayings, not easily to be received? Doubtless in one view they are. Would you have had a wider constituency for Christ, embracing all without distinction, and so secured the salvation of all? But God has made His own plan, and if Jesus fell in with that plan, and saw of the travail of His soul in its fulfillment, it is surely not for us to quarrel with it. There are things too deep for us in these arrangements. As Vinet remarks, there is a mystery of grace, and there is a mystery of liberty. It is certain that there if no limitation in the offer of the gospel. Bright and clear the inscription stands over the gate of heaven: "Whosoever will, let him take the water of life freely." The invitation of Jesus knows no restriction: "Come unto me, all ye that labour and are heavy laden, and I will give you rest." And the reason which Jesus assigns for men not coming is simply their own unwillingness: "Ye will not come to me, that ye might have life."

Have we come to Christ, then, or have we not? If not, why not? Only because we are not willing. Can we, then, reasonably complain of not getting what we are not willing to take? Or have we been led to see that the root of the evil is our unwillingness, and that God only can deal effectually with that? Are we lying at His feet, helpless, and appealing to Him to loosen the chain that hinders our coming? No man ever lay long in such an attitude uncared for. The wistful look of the helpless soul is a look that God cannot disregard; the hands stretched out to Him are never stretched in vain. Only there is a fear of our not taking in the simple answer. God bids us trust all our interests to His Son, in whom all fulness dwells; fulness of power to break our chain as well as pardon our sin, to give liberty to the captives and the opening of the prison to them that are bound.

But have you entered within the gates of grace, and found in Christ the life and blessing you desired? Look back, and see the inscriptions *inside* the gates. "Ye have not chosen me, but I have chosen you." "Even when we were dead in sins, God hath quickened us together with Christ." "According as he hath chosen us in him before the foundation of the world." "Having predestinated us to the adoption of children by Jesus Christ unto himself." Your redemption has originated in a Divine purpose. The position you are now in has been reached, not through your own feeble efforts, but through the strong hand of God upon you. Now you. see how true it is that the sympathetic Savior has taken up your case, and has dealt with it as if it were His own. Had it not been so, how should your sleep in sin have been disturbed, your heart made willing, your chains broken, your feet set on the rock? Is not all this the result of the loving sympathy and care of your Redeemer, of Him who took you up into His heart, and charged Himself with all your interests? And may you not well rely with all confidence on the continuance of that process which owes its beginning to such wonderful grace? Only, on your part, let there be some fitting response to Him who has loved you, and washed you from your sins in His own blood. Let the question be asked that is so meet: "Lord, what wilt thou have me to do? "And let your conversation correspond to your privileges. For "ye are a chosen generation, a royal priesthood, a holy nation, a peculiar people, that ye should show forth the praises of him who hath called you out of darkness into his marvellous light."

HIS SORROWS

"A man of sorrows, and acquainted with grief." — Isaiah 53.3

There is no reason to doubt the truth of the current tradition that when our Lord was crucified He had not passed His thirty- fourth year. He had still the dew of His youth upon Him. No natural process of decay had begun to diminish His strength or to depress His spirits. Yet it needs not to be shown that He had felt a burden of sorrow so heavy and so peculiar, that it was like to no other sorrow. The prophet's expression is not too strong; He was "a man of sorrows." His life was not indeed all sorrow; He had His fountains of joy, very sweet and very refreshing; but a deep current of sorrow ran through it, and gave it a characteristic tinge. We cannot attach much weight to any so-called likeness of Christ that has either floated down to us by tradition, or been devised by the painter's imagination; yet it is a significant fact that nothing was ever presented as a likeness of Christ that did not show deep lines of sadness. And in looking for the causes of His grief, we are not left to mere mysterious surmisings or vague impressions. Some of the elements, indeed, we cannot fully analyze or comprehend, but much of it lies within our ken; and the careful consideration of it is well fitted, under God's blessing, to bring Christ nearer to us, and give us a clearer conception both of His life and of His work.

1. In trying to bring into view some of the leading sorrows of our Lord's life, it is impossible not to begin with one which lay at the bottom of them all — that, namely, which arose from *His close contact with the sin and defilement of this fallen and guilty world*.

The fact of our Lord's becoming a man involved the necessity of His living in immediate contact with what of all things in the universe was the most repulsive, hateful, and horrible to His soul. "Thou art of purer eyes than to behold evil, and canst not look on iniquity," said the prophet Habakkuk; and this striking statement was as true of the second Person as of the first or the third.

When, therefore, the second Person took upon Him the form of a servant, and was made in the likeness of man, it became necessary for Him to live in fearfully close contact with that which excited His supreme and infinite abhorrence. We may perhaps get some faint conception of what this implied by illustrations derived from our own experience, but the full magnitude of the trial passes our powers of conception. Set a person remarkable for cleanliness to live in some Hottentot kraal, or in an encampment of tinkers; you know the life of perpetual disgust which imprisonment in so filthy a den must involve. Place a young man of high principle and purity in a gang of gamblers and swindlers; let him hear for the first time all that he venerates bespattered with the coarsest ridicule; let the oath and the unclean jest, let the yell of passion and the chuckle of successful villany be the sounds that ordinarily fall on his ear; can you conceive a deeper horror or a blacker despair than that which falls on him as he thinks how he is doomed to this lot, he cannot tell for how long? Now, when Christ came to live among men, He exposed Himself to a similar but far deeper horror. He came to live in a world that was in rebellion against its Lord. This was true of all by nature; true of Jew and Gentile, Barbarian, Scythian, bond and free. This alone was a terrible fact. It needed not that all men should be murderers or robbers to excite repulsion in the mind of Jesus. It was enough that all were in rebellion against Him whose will was to Him the symbol of all that was venerable, and claimed the most implicit submission. It was enough that God had cause to say of all, "I have nourished and brought up children, and they have rebelled against me."

Who can tell all the pain that passed through the pure heart of Jesus at the perpetual sight of the world's rebellion? No doubt there were many beautiful things in the world, and even in men's lives, that could not but interest Him; but there was an awful drawback in the case of all. It was a world in arms against its Lord, a world divorced from its God. Even where appearances were fairest, the trail of the serpent might readily be seen — the defilement and destruction of his poisonous slime. Nothing was absolutely pure, and in most places the visible disorder was terrible. How could Jesus put up with it? How could He compose Himself to live calmly and to work patiently in such a world? There can be no doubt that it must have cost Him a great effort of self-restraint. If, for the sake of doing good, the most delicately nurtured girl in our country were to become an inmate of the lowest hovel in London or Edinburgh, what an effort of self-restraint it would cost her to suppress her disgust, and go about patiently cleansing, and mending, and nursing, and teaching, and trying in every way to throw order and sunshine into the wretched place!

Even this illustration gives us but a faint conception of the restraint to which Jesus must have subjected Himself in order to go about and do His work in this world at all. He must have found it necessary to shut His eyes for a time to that aspect of the world, so as not to allow it always to engross His attention and paralyze His heart. Now, this was very different from the effect which familiarity with vice often produces. Familiarity with vice often blinds the eyes to its character as vice, makes men think little of it, and by-and-by reconciles them to the practice of it themselves. Need we say that in the case of Jesus there was and there could be no such effect; no familiarity with vice could ever make Him think lightly of rebellion against the will of God.

But it is quite another thing to keep one's feelings in abeyance for a time, as many a parent has to do, living with a dissipated son; as many others have to do when in daily contact with persons of incorrigible wickedness. It becomes a necessity for such persons to keep their feelings in check during the ordinary intercourse of the day; but only, when solitude comes, to pour them out the more freely in humiliation and prayer to God. Such persons know that if their feelings were always loose and free they would be unable to apply themselves to work, — they would be quite overcome; and they learn to place them for a time, as it were, under lock and key.

So, we believe, Jesus must have done. But just as with others the suppression of the feelings by day is often followed by the more vehement outpouring of them by night; so, in His case, the nights spent alone, the nights spent in prayer upon the mountains, would bear ample testimony to the depth of His distress. Often, doubtless, would He take up the words of the Psalmist: "Rivers of waters run down mine eyes, because they keep not thy law. Trouble and anguish hath taken hold of me: yet thy commandments are my delights."

The grief to which we have now adverted would have been much the same whatever the purpose for which Jesus had come into the world. But we go on to note a sorrow that arose especially out of the most gracious, loving errand He came to fulfill, and that must have added immeasurably to the burden of His grief.

2. It is *the sorrow of unrequited love*. "He came to his own, and his own received him not." He came with balm of Gilead to a stricken world, and they would have none of Him or His balm. He came to the people that, of all the tribes of the earth, might have been expected to welcome him; to whose fathers he had so often drawn nigh, as the Angel of the Covenant, in their hours of darkness; by whose prophets triumphal arches had been reared in His honor, and branches of palm trees scattered along the whole line of His progress; and for whose sakes, that there might be no room for mistake, He had shadowed forth His higher blessings by healing the sick, cleansing the lepers, casting out devils, giving sight to the blind, and raising the dead. Yet in the sacred capital of this country the cry arose, "Away with him, crucify him;" and in a place of skulls, an accursed place — all the more marked because so near the holy city — He was fastened to a cross and openly murdered before God and man.

Now we all know that there is something very sad in the repulse of a generous love, a love that seeks truly and disinterestedly the welfare of those loved; and further, we learn from Scripture that the rejection of His loving offers cut very deeply into the heart of Jesus.

It is a favorite figure of the prophets to compare Israel to a wayward and treacherous wife that had trifled with the affections of her Divine husband, and taken up with lovers that did not even pretend to any genuine love for her. Whatever in this connection is most pathetic in the lamentations of Jeremiah and Hosea over treacherous Israel and her equally treacherous sister Judah, was but the foreshadow of that crushing sorrow which filled the heart of Jesus when the Jews would not have Him as their Savior. Who can estimate the anguish of His heart, loving them so tenderly, and knowing so well what their sins deserved, when they would not have His remedy — would not come to Him that they might have life? Who can estimate the bitterness of His pain, when, looking forward to that crowning act of national rejection so soon to be consummated, he said, "O Jerusalem, Jerusalem, thou that killest the prophets, and stonest them which are sent unto thee, how often would I have gathered thy children together, as a hen gathereth her chickens under her wings; and ye would not."

It is quite true that the blessed Lord is to "see of the travail of his soul and be satisfied." It is not to be disappointment in the end. "All that the Father giveth me," He said, truly, "shall come to me;" or as the apostle puts it, "whom he did predestinate, them he also called:

and whom he called, them he also justified: and whom he justified, them he also glorified." We get into a very difficult region when we begin to lay God's purposes alongside Christ's feelings. Perhaps the adjustment of them is the most difficult question that can be raised. In one sense, beyond doubt, the blessed Lord was satisfied with the results of His work, because it fulfilled the Father's plan; and the Son knew well that whatever the Father planned must be infinitely wise and merciful and good. But in a more human sense Jesus had many bitter disappointments in His work. His human feelings were most grievously hurt. It was sad to stand at the door knocking, knocking, knocking, and meet with no response. It was sad to stand till His head was filled with dew, and His locks with the drops of the night. It cut very deep that those whom He loved would not open the door. What sunshine could He have shed into the dwelling! But they would not have the pardon which He offered them from the Father. They would not have the new heart, nor the new home, nor the new inheritance. They preferred Egypt to Canaan. They would linger in Sodom though the fiery flood was ready to come down on it. Alas for them when that flood should come! The thought of it was more than He could bear. "And when he was come near, he beheld the city, and wept over it, saying. If thou hadst known, even thou, at least in this thy day, the things which belong unto thy peace! but now they are hid from thine eyes."

3. But Jesus had a great deal more to grieve Him than the neglect or refusal of His love. A third grief arose from what is called, in the Epistle to the Hebrews, *the contradiction of sinners against Himself*.

He had to encounter a great amount of keen, active opposition, often of a peculiarly trying kind. Hardly was He born when the King of the Jews sent out his band of licensed murderers to kill him. The obscurity of Nazareth sheltered Him for a time; but when He came out as a public man, even His own townsmen dragged Him towards a precipice to throw Him headlong down. His works of mercy were ascribed to Beelzebub. He Himself was charged at one time with having a devil, at another time with being mad. The scribes and Pharisees, the religious leaders of the nation, came to Him again and again, tempting Him, that they might entangle Him in His talk. The Pharisees joined for this purpose with their mortal enemies, the Sadducees. The Herodians too, were set up by some of them to try their arts upon Him. Looking at the number and variety of His enemies, He might have said, "They compassed me about like bees." Hardly ever did He undertake an unembarrassed journey, or spend an easy hour. Was it not hard to have all this to bear in an enterprise of mercy, and to have to bear it from the very persons whom He was eager to bless?

It is said that He *endured* this contradiction, as if it were a thing peculiarly hard and wearing. It is sufficiently trying, when one undertakes a work of mercy, to have one's intentions misunderstood at the beginning, and to be accused of a desire to benefit one's self, though the accusation from its very absurdity may answer itself. But in such a case, one trusts that time will clear the air; that the real purpose for which one is laboring will become apparent; and however a few interested persons may persevere in their spiteful opposition, the public generally will form a true judgment of one's aim. But to our blessed Lord the contradiction of sinners became only more intense the longer He labored. And it was the more trying because it was so successful. Two processes went on together. Wherever He was unimpeded, wherever He had free course, His blessed errand was appreciated; men called Him "the son of David," and even at Jerusalem many cut down branches from the trees and threw their garments on the road and shouted "Hosanna!" But alongside this process there went on the contradiction of sinners; and plots and calumnies, cunning insinuations and shameless lies, freely poured against Him, did their evil work. As His hour approached, it became apparent that this contradiction of sinners was to carry the day. Yet Jesus endured it. Worrying though it was. He never lost His self-possession under it; it was part of His cup; and "the cup which my Father hath given me, shall I not drink it?"

Amid these griefs and worries, how did it fare with Christ in the immediate circle of His friends? On the whole, no doubt, it fared well; the companionship of the twelve was a comfort. "Ye are they," He could say of them, "that have continued with me in my temptations." But it was not a uniform comfort. It had its drawbacks, and these drawbacks were of such a kind as to add materially to the griefs of Jesus.

4. Among His sorrows, therefore, we notice, fourthly, those which came from *the infirmities of His own disciples*. The instances of these, narrated in the Gospels, show that, both in number and in kind, they must have sensibly contributed to the vexations of Jesus; not, however, habitually, but occasionally. Thus, there were vexations arising from their want of understanding, want of sympathy with Him in the great

purposes of His life. At one time they were for forbidding a man to cast out devils because he did not follow with them. At another they were for calling down fire from heaven to consume a village of the Samaritans. They were for Jesus doing small things, revolting to His magnanimity; and harsh things, repulsive to His love.

Then there were disappointments, arising from their want of faith and of the courage of faith. "O thou of little faith, wherefore didst thou doubt?" was the rebuke to Peter when he got frightened on the sea; as it was the rebuke conveyed on a more awful occasion, when the cock crew and the Lord looked upon Peter. There were vexations caused by their paltry strifes and worldly ambitions; by their disputing with one another who should be the greatest; and by their asking for the chief places in His kingdom. There were vexations arising from their utter unfitness to meet the great crisis of His own life; the three sleeping in the garden being but the prelude to the whole taking flight in the hour of His apprehension, and shrinking from Him as He hung on the cross. Lastly, there was the treachery of Judas — an act which entered deeply into Christ's soul, and drew out one of His bitterest groans. To find desertion where He might have looked for protection, and treachery instead of fidelity; to be betrayed with a kiss, to be entrapped with words of apparent affection, was an awful trial. To be sold by one of His own disciples for thirty pieces of silver, as it was the climax of His degradation, so it marked the bitterest pang that was ever inflicted on His heart by the hand of man. It was the cruelest wound in the house of His friends.

5. We come now to the last of the especial griefs of Jesus — the sorrow of His last conflict; the grief, so peculiar and so intense, of what He often called His hour. It is apparent, from all the records of His life, that our blessed Lord looked forward to His last span of life as one of peculiar horror. "I have a baptism to be baptized with," He said, "and how am I straitened till it be accomplished!" Like a person in ill health looking forward to a dreadful surgical operation; like an innocent person, accused of a crime, looking forward to the day of the trial; so, but with far deeper emotion, did Jesus look forward to His hour. To meet this hour demanded all His powers of endurance: when the time drew nigh for Him to be offered up. He had to set His face steadfastly to go up to Jerusalem. The token that the hour had come was a somewhat peculiar one: it was hearing that certain Greeks had been inquiring for Him. Gratifying in itself, this was the signal of an awful crisis, and He cried out in deep soul-trouble, eager, if it had

been only possible, to find deliverance. The same feeling took deep hold on Him in Gethsemane, and it cast its shadow on Him as He hung on the cross.

What could have been the nature of this unexampled feeling? Guided by the whole tenor of Scripture, the Christian Church has ever seen but one possible explanation; that at this solemn crisis of His life, more than at any other part of it, it was His lot to feel the position of the sin-bearer and the scapegoat — the position of One who stood in the sinner's place and bore the sinner's doom. It was then that God said, "Awake, O sword, against my shepherd, and against the man that is my fellow, saith the Lord of hosts." The whole circumstances of the case were terrible. To be dragged like a criminal through the streets; to be driven beyond the sacred city; to be consigned to an unclean place; to be visited with the malefactor's doom; to be betrayed by one apostle, denied by another, and forsaken by all; to be cast off, as it were, by universal humanity; to have not one brother, or lover, or friend, or follower near; and then to have this awful sentence of man's against Him, confirmed, as it were, by God; to feel that all the stripes of God and man were tearing Him, as if He had been guilty of all the world's sin; oh, it was a darkness and a bitterness infinitely beyond our comprehension: it was an experience by itself in the history of the world! No wonder though it troubled Him to look forward to it; no wonder though He shivered as He felt its shadow; no wonder though He staggered when the cloud burst over His head. Yet this most memorable condition of His Messiahship must have been full in His view when He undertook the office of Mediator. This, too, the Son of God deliberately resolved to encounter, and included in the terms of His acceptance of His office. "Lo, I come, I delight to do thy will, O my God!"

And now what are we to think of all this? Is it not a solemn fact that our Lord's visit to this world was so sad a visit? Not uniformly, or always, sad — as we shall have occasion to show a little further on, when we proceed to consider his joys. But still it was very markedly sad, and sad in consequence of what we were, and what we did. Can we suppose that if, out of great kindness, a friend came to pay us a visit at our home, and if his visit was a very sad one, we should be unaffected by the thought? If he was sad when he saw how we were living; sad because we would not receive his loving offers; sad because he had been worried all the time, more or less, by contumely and opposition; sad because even we, his friends, had either turned against him or refused to stand by him; and if there were other and still deeper causes of distress to him, it cannot be that we would be unmoved. If we could not but admit these facts, should we not be vexed at ourselves for our treatment of our friend?

Does it mend the case, then, that it was the Son of God that came on an errand of mercy to our world? *We*, indeed, were not there, but we were represented by those that were there, and our hearts are not different from their hearts. Have we then not virtually contributed to the load of our Savior's griefs? And shall we not be humbled by the fact? Shall we hold our heads high, and think how well it would be if other people were like us, while, in fact, we have helped to grieve the soul of Jesus? Shall we go on laughing and rollicking like the careless world, never heeding the sad look on that fairest of faces, or the groan over us from those lips that drop like the honeycomb?

Surely we will not go on adding to our guilt by rejecting the loving offers of Christ! We will not break His heart by our cold indifference, and reject the love that would seek and save us! We dare not brave for ourselves the awful doom of sin, when we see how terrible it was for Christ to bear it! We will not refuse His invitation to the feast of Divine love and grace, when we know how it would delight Him to see us in His festive hall, and what a welcome we should receive from Him there!

At once, then, let us resolve that Christ shall be our Savior. He deserves our heart, and He shall have it; He deserves our life, and He shall have it. Would only that He would so draw us to Him that we would run after Him; and so keep us united to Him that His love would ever warm our hearts, and His strength fit us for all the duties and trials of the Christian life!

HIS PEACE

"Peace I leave with you; my peace I give unto you." —
John 14.27

The perfect self-possession of our blessed Lord, the habitual calm of His spirit, the absence of fever and flutter, even when He was most burdened with responsibility and worried with contradiction, are features that arrest every eye. We see Him calm in every difficulty, ready in every emergency, unruffled in every conflict. The rude interruptions encountered in delivering His discourses or performing His miracles He meets with combined dignity and courtesy; and though He has sometimes a sharp word for the perversity of His apostles, and even an indignant burst at the hypocrisy of the Pharisees, His soul does not lose its composure; He is presently calm and benignant as ever. The miracle of calming the sea seems symbolical of His whole life:

winds and waves are ever failing before Him; wherever He goes there is peace and calm.

Is it this peace that He bequeaths to His people when He says, "Peace I leave with you, my peace I give unto you"? What a blessed legacy it must be! Is it possible for us to lead a life where, amid all that may be outwardly boisterous, there is inward tranquility like His? Who would not learn the secret of such a life? Who would not be heir to One who promises such a legacy?

We must observe, however, that there are two senses in which the peace here promised may be called Christ's. It may be called His because He has procured it; it is the fruit of His work, the result of His atonement, and of the blessed relation to the Father into which all who believe are brought by Him. Or it may be called Christ's peace for the more especial reason that has just been adverted to: because it is the peace which He personally enjoyed; that which dwelt in His own human soul; that which made His human life the picture of serenity which all feel that it was. In both these senses Jesus gives peace to His believing people. In the one sense it is the peace of justification, in the other of sanctification; the first arises from a new relation, the second from a new character; and both come through union to Him, the sole source of all saving blessings.

"Peace" is often used in the former of these senses, as the result of Christ's redeeming work. "Being justified by faith, we have peace with God through our Lord Jesus Christ." Sin has made a feud between us and God; it has exposed us to the just displeasure of the righteous One; it has taught us to tremble at the very mention of our Father's name. But Jesus has suffered, the just for the unjust, to bring us unto God; He has redeemed us from the curse of the law, being made a curse for us. Under cover of His righteousness we do not dread the penalty of disobedience; being justified by faith, the feud that separated us from God is healed. We see Him in Christ, reconciling the world unto Himself, and not imputing their trespasses unto them. There is no screen now between us and our Father's love. He is faithful and just to forgive us our sins, and to cleanse us from all unrighteousness. To know this, and to rest on it, is peace.

And in no other way is there real peace for sinful man. He cannot look into God's face, and feel that He is a Father, pouring out on him His everlasting love, except through faith in the redemption of Christ. None of us can have boldness to enter into the holiest of all but by the blood of Jesus; and no comfort can be more than a superficial and changeable emotion which does not rest on the foundation of Israel's thanksgiving: "O Lord, I will praise thee; though thou wast angry with me, thine anger is turned away, and thou comfortest me."

But it is the other sense of the term that we have to do with in inquiring into the inner life of our Lord. We are called to view the peace which He left to His disciples as His own, as the peace that reigned in His own heart. He imparts to them a precious secret of which He had Himself exemplified the virtue, and which in their coming days of trial would have the like effect upon them.

Can we then, in any measure, analyze this peace which was so beautiful in the human life of Jesus? If it was an attribute of His human soul, it must have had its roots in His relation as a man to the Father, Heavenly as its effects were, it must have come from God. Can we find the sources of the stream? Can we see anything in the relation which Jesus as a man sustained to His Father, that, in accounting for His peace, will, at the same time, point the way to ours?

1. To a large extent the peace of Christ's soul is accounted for by His oneness with the Father, and especially by the entire submission of His human will to the control of the Father's.

We have seen already how much of the strife and turmoil of human life is due to the collision of wills. We have seen that even the collision of human wills produces endless trouble, and that when a human will comes into collision with the Divine will, the resulting strife is fearful. On the other hand, in every social relation where there is unity of will there is peace and concord; and where there is unity of will between man and God, the peace that follows is unspeakably glorious. In the case of Jesus, unity of will with the Father was the natural condition of His life. Not only, therefore, was the most prolific source of disturbance absent from Him, but the sweetest cause of tranquility was in full operation. To resign His will to the Father's, to give up His own, or what might have been His own, when the Father's was different, was not to Him a lesson which He had learned amid the pain and sorrow of many a bootless conflict; the habit had formed itself from the dawn of consciousness, and had all the ease and force of a natural operation.

Through life, therefore, He had the calm and pleasant feeling that nothing could happen to Him that was not in harmony with that will which was infinitely holy and wise and good. Things might happen which were deeply painful, but nothing could happen that was not right. Of some things that were essential to the work which He had undertaken, the pain might be excessive; but even that was all under the control of the Father, and would eventually work for good. As the waves and billows passed over His head, it might sometimes seem as if it were impossible that God could have ordained things so hard to bear; but ere long a point would be reached where it would be seen that all the paths of the Lord were mercy and truth to such as kept His covenant. Who can fathom the depths of that peace which must have habitually come to Jesus from this perfect harmony of will with the Father, or comprehend the repose of the soul that could thus lean on the support of the everlasting arms?

2. From the oneness of will between Jesus and the Father there sprung *a spirit of confidence* which swept

away many of the troubles of life. By trusting the Father, Jesus was able to rid Himself of anxieties and perplexities that disturb the tranquility of many a life. Two classes of such anxieties are adverted to by Himself. The former and more superficial are those connected with what we shall eat and what we shall drink and wherewithal we shall be clothed. If He deemed it enough, in dealing with such anxieties in the case of others, to refer to the lilies and the ravens, we may believe that no deeper argument was needed by Himself. With all the force and ease of an intuitive conviction, the sight of these objects would assure Him that there was no cause whatever for fretting about the common necessaries of life. No perverse spirit of distrust would arise to counteract the simple and conclusive argument. We are liable to fancy that, armed as Jesus was with supernatural power, He never could have felt the temptation to anxiety as we do, because He had always that power to fall back on if things should come to extremities. But never did Jesus fall back on His miraculous powers, or feel that He was entitled to use them for any such purpose. He who, at the beginning of His career, refused to use His power for turning the stones of the desert into bread, refused to use it at the end of His career for producing the few drops of water that would have been such a boon when He said on the cross, "I thirst!" Beyond all doubt, it was from the lilies and the ravens that Jesus drew the spirit that reposed so calmly on the goodness of Providence, and drove to such a distance all temporal anxieties. As it was apparent from their case that no creature, however insignificant, while fulfilling the purpose of God in its creation, was left without its appropriate sustenance; so it was certain that God's own children, while fulfilling the far higher objects of their being, would never be left without food and clothing. Anxiety on such topics, reaching to a troubled and painful perplexity, would have involved a reflection on the fatherly character of God. It never disturbed the peace of Jesus, and as little need it harass the minds of His people.

But there are other perplexities, far more terrible than these, to which the human spirit lies exposed. This class of perplexities concerns the rectitude of God's doings. It sometimes seems as if the Judge of all the earth were not doing justly. His ways have the appearance of

not being even. He does things that seem to be incompatible with infinite generosity and love. There are no subjects that are more apt to trouble His children. Sometimes the perplexities arise in their own minds, and sometimes they are forced harshly upon their notice by the jibes and taunts of objectors. How did Jesus act or feel with reference to such subjects of perplexity? No doubt His human soul could see through difficulties of this kind much farther than we can. Many things that are dark to us were not dark to Him. On some awful topics where we can only speak with trembling lip His utterance was clear and authoritative. Yet Jesus lets us understand that on certain deep questions, involving the rectitude of God's ways, He simply fell back on the spirit of trust. It is a perplexing question why any of the sons of men are allowed to come short of eternal life. Why does the light of the gospel not shine with such commanding and controlling luster as to fill every eye and convert every soul? Why does the gospel often prove unsuccessful with men of culture and intelligence, whose subtle faculties would seem so well fitted to apprehend its excellence? Why, in a word, are the things of salvation often hid from the wise and prudent, while they are revealed to babes? Our blessed Lord does not seek to escape from this perplexity through any outlet peculiar to Himself. He does not attempt to solve the problem. He comes to rest in regard to it simply through trust in the Father. He gets rid of perplexity by shutting His eyes, and thinking how certain it is, in spite of all appearance to the contrary, that the Father will do right. "Even so, Father: for so it seemed good in thy sight" (Matthew 11.25, 26).

"Lord, my heart is not haughty, nor mine eyes lofty: neither do I exercise myself in great matters, or in things too great for me. Surely I have behaved and quieted myself, as a child that is weaned of his mother: my soul is even as a weaned child. Let Israel hope in the Lord from henceforth and for ever" (Psalm 131).

How touching and beautiful to find the blessed Lord solving His difficult problems by the spirit of trust in His Father, and coming thus to rest! How instructive for us to know that much of the peace and serenity of His soul was due to this process! And in His case it was not the resource of the baffled mind that, after wearying itself as in the very fire to solve all difficulties, is compelled by dire necessity to fall back on this position. In the case of Jesus, it is the position taken up at first and at once, in reference to questions that are intuitively seen to he beyond the depth of the human mind. We do not say that, to all minds, precisely the same questions will always appear to belong to this category. But we may surely say, with the example of Jesus before us, that there will always be questions on which it is rash and wrong for the human spirit to give judgment, or to assume a positive tone. In reference to these, it is not merely the part of wisdom, but it is essential to our peace and tranquility, that in the spirit of filial trust we leave them in the hands of One above us. "Even so. Father: for so it seemed good in thy sight."

3. Another element that contributed to our Lord's peace was His meek and lowly temper. "Learn of me, for I am meek and lowly in heart, *and ye shall find rest to your souls.*" It does not need much observation to see how many of our troubles arise from our carrying our heads too high, expecting too much from other men, and chafing and fretting when we do not meet with the consideration which we looked for. To a man of the proud temper of Haman. it is torture that a single human being, one miserable Mordecai, refuses him the homage on which he has set his heart. A proud ambitious temper is the prolific source of irritation and discontent. Even where there may be little of conscious pride, the subtle feeling that makes self its idol is constantly offended when the idol is treated with indifference. And when men begin to seek great things for themselves and for their families, they are not willing to trust themselves to the providence of God. They have a secret feeling that God does not sympathize with them in their ambition; and therefore it is not enough to trust to what He may be willing to do for them. They walk in a vain show, they are disquieted in vain. They rise up early, they sit up late, land eat the bread of sorrows.

Offenses that might easily be overlooked are cherished, and where no offense was intended, offense is often taken. Alas, that high-minded temper; of what endless troubles it is the cause! The bites and stings of venomous insects, in a tropical country, do not irritate the skin to the same extent as the actings of a proud, sensitive, ambitious temper fret and fever the soul.

But the blessed Lord lived far from all these things. He sought not honor from men. It mattered little to Him personally how men regarded Him. He had made up His mind to bear whatever treatment He might receive. He had no ambitious projects, no style that must be maintained, no. appearances that must be kept up. His only treatment of injuries and offenses was to forgive them. They never tarried in His breast, to swell and fester and irritate. All such things were foreign to His nature. Love was so busy and so full that no bitter feeling could get a foothold in His heart. Humility was so ready with her gentle and soothing ways, that Pride, with his fierce looks and high words, could never get within. Even in His kingly glory the meekness of His spirit appears: "Behold, thy King cometh unto thee, meek, and sitting upon an ass, even a colt, the foal of an ass."

It hardly needs to be pointed out in what close connection this meek and lowly spirit of Jesus stood to the great purpose of His life. "The Son of man came not to be ministered unto, but to minister, and to give his life a ransom for many." Had He come to be ministered unto, with the purpose to exact from all men such homage as was due to Him, He would not have exhibited the same meek and lowly spirit. He would not have given that meek answer when they who gathered the temple-tribute came to ask it of Him. He would not have met the treachery of Judas with the calm question, "Betrayest thou the Son of man with a kiss?" As it was, the offensive treatment He received from men did not ordinarily interfere with the great purpose of His life. It deprived Him of nothing on which His heart was set. His heart was set on ministering, healing sorrow, creating joy, overcoming evil with good. Calmly pursuing these objects. He viewed with comparative indifference the scorn and antagonism of the world. In the lowly sphere of loving service He kept Himself free from a thousand irritations, and had for His daily companion "the peace of God that passeth all understanding."

"Learn of me," He may well say to us, "for I am meek and lowly of heart." But if we would have His lowly temper, we must adopt His characteristic purpose of life.

It is not easy by sheer force to subdue passions so strong as pride and ambition, or even the ordinary temper of a self-seeking heart. But if, in sympathy with Jesus, we fall in love with a ministering life, the process will become far easier. Things fall more readily into order when we have a practical object the pursuit of which deeply interests us. If we lay ourselves out for usefulness; if it becomes the chief pleasure of our heart to make the crooked straight, and the rough places plain; if it be a joy to us "to make a sunshine in the shady place;" if we are willing to accept as gifts from God any worldly advantages and honors which come to our lot, or are reconciled to the want of them by the thought that it has not seemed good to Him to give them; then we shall be entering into the spirit of Christ, we shall be taking His yoke on us and learning of Him who was meek and lowly in heart; and finding His yoke easy and His burden light, we shall obtain rest to our souls.

4. Our Lord indicates, as another source of His peace, the abiding presence of His Father. "Behold, the hour cometh," He said in His farewell discourse, "yea, is now come, that ye shall be scattered, every one to his own, and shall leave me alone: and yet I am not alone, because the Father is with me" (John 16.32). The gracious presence of the Father, known and felt as a

reality, especially in times of trial, was, we may believe, the crowning support of His heart, and the deepest fountain of His peace. "Whom have I in heaven but thee, and there is none upon earth that I desire beside thee. My flesh and my heart faileth, but God is the strength of my heart, and my portion for ever." We know that this fellowship with the Father was maintained through constant prayer; and in the intercessory prayer of His last evening, we see how intimate the fellowship was, and of what a peace-bringing kind. Nothing can be more real than the communion there represented, and nothing more soothing than the tone in which it is maintained. No better commentary could be found on His own words, "Yet I am not alone, because the Father is with me;" nor could any experience more vividly fulfill the promise, "Thou wilt keep him in perfect peace whose mind is stayed on thee, because he trusteth in thee."

Perhaps there is nothing which carnal men are less willing to believe in than the reality of God's especial presence with earnest believers. To them it seems presumption for any man to say that God is with him more than He is with all men who are living in a creditable way. It savors of fanaticism and fancifulness to represent any feelings of theirs as sure signs of the presence of God. And beyond all doubt, this is a matter on which it becomes every man to speak but little, and to speak with care. But does not the experience of the Master prove the reality of the privilege? For since our Lord said, "As I am, so are ye in this world," surely in this great privilege the servant may share. If it was real to the Master, it may be real to the servant. The experience of our blessed Lord is for our encouragement and example. To us, as to Him, it is possible to say, "I have set the Lord always before me; because he is at my right hand I shall not be moved." And it is only what all Church history testifies, that the men who have known most of God's presence are likewise the men who have known most of peace.

Of all the elements of true peace, the most important is a sure foundation. Of all hollow cries, the hollowest is, "Peace, peace, when there is no peace." But to get peace from the hands of Jesus is ample guarantee for its genuineness. To get the peace which He enjoyed — peace derived from oneness with the Father, from trust in all that He is and does, from the exercise of a lowly, ministering spirit, and from the conscious presence of God with us — is to get the peace of God that passeth all understanding, and that keeps the heart and mind through Christ Jesus.

HIS JOY

"These things have I spoken unto you, that my joy might remain in you, and that your joy might be full." — John 15.11

Joy is an attribute with which our minds are somewhat unwilling to clothe our Lord. The common impression is that He hardly knew what joy means. Joy, as every one knows, is an emotion that shows itself in good spirits, radiant looks, and cheerful tones; it is the result of a satisfaction that swells the soul; it is a pleasure that excites our nature, that raises our spirits above the ordinary level. We shout for joy, we leap for joy, we sing for joy. Now it is not easy for us to think of our blessed Lord having ever in His public life had any experience like this. The sorrows that He had to bear were so heavy that we can hardly think of Him in any frame of mind of which sadness was not the prevailing element. At first sight it seems impossible that our Lord could ever have felt otherwise than oppressed with the burden of the world's sin, and the punishment of it which He had to bear. We have not the same difficulty in thinking of peace as an attribute of His soul. In fact, our common impression of the state of Christ's spirit is, that it was one of tranquil resignation, of meek submission to nameless horrors. But that He ever had times of joy — jubilant seasons in which He appeared to lose sight of His sorrows, and to be borne along by bright and happy thoughts — seems hardly compatible with the work which He came to do.

Yet it appears from His own words that He was no stranger to joy. Life to Him had one side awfully dark: its shadow often fell on Him, and was never far off: but life to Him had a bright side also, and there was an elasticity of nature about Him that enabled Him to enter at due times into this experience too. For it is not characteristic of the highest natures to be always in one mood. It is not a mark of greatness to be for ever looking on one side of things. In the healthy soul there is a springy power that resists the pressure of the heaviest load, and finds relief in other directions — in occupying itself with other thoughts. It was a sign of the greatness of Christ's soul that He rose at times above all the depressing influences of His unexampled position.

Probably our impression of His unchanging sadness is a legacy from the Church of Rome. The type of devotion which that Church labors most to foster is not radiant, but gloomy; not joyous, but grievous. The sight of Jesus with which it commonly fills the eye of its worshippers is that of Jesus in agony, Jesus on the cross, Jesus with all the marks of physical torture, sweating the bloody sweat, crowned with thorns, pierced by nails, swollen with blows, broken with manifold anguish. But this is only one side of the truth. There must have been times when Jesus was radiant and happy, otherwise how should He have attracted little children as He did? How should He have been so social in His habits, so much in the society of His fellows, instead of courting seclusion, as grief ever does? How should He have been so habitually ready for His work, so quickly refreshed after labors, so full of activity and life? How should He have been such a contrast to John the Baptist, who came neither eating nor drinking, and who seems to have looked very much on the dark side of life? How should He have told His disciples that fasting was not appropriate for them while He was among them; that while the bridegroom was with them they had cause rather for festive feelings; and that it would be the time to mourn when the bridegroom should be taken away? All this points to a bright side of Christ's earthly life. It is not for us to settle the proportion between the dark and the bright in His experience. But we seem to be warranted in believing that while the ordinary level of His soul was that of peaceful composure, there were times at which it was especially depressed by grief, and times also at which it was elevated by joy. The one experience seems to have balanced the other. And Jesus seems to have verified the truth of Nehemiah's maxim, that the joy of the Lord is the strength of His people.

What, then, was the nature of Christ's joy? and from what sources was it derived?

Perhaps it would be enough to answer this question in the words of a single verse of Scripture: "Thou lovest righteousness, and hatest wickedness: *therefore* God, thy God, hath anointed thee with the oil of gladness above thy fellows " (Psalm 45.7). By a Divine law, His love of righteousness and hatred of wickedness distilled on His soul a larger share of the oil of gladness than fell on any of His fellows. The holiness or wholeness of His nature, the healthiness or haleness of His soul (for all these words are from the same root, and have a similar meaning), the perfect order of everything within. His thorough conformity to the Divine rule of rectitude, caused Him to experience a gladness beyond the measure of other men. We may note an analogy here between the body and the soul. When the body is in perfect health, there is a sensation of joy in the very play of its organs, as we see in children and the young of animals; there is an exuberance of delight that finds ready outlets in many characteristic ways. But when disease impairs an organ, or interferes with its natural action, instead of joy there is heaviness and pain. The case is similar with the soul. When the soul is disordered by sin its action is heavy and painful. But when it is in full health, when all its faculties are in order, and are devoted freely to their proper objects, especially the highest, there is exquisite joy in their action.

Now in the human soul of Jesus there was no trace of disorder; all the machinery worked smoothly and sweetly; every faculty was directed to its appropriate end. Hence His reflex enjoyment. "God, even thy God, hath anointed thee with the oil of gladness above thy fellows."

Passing, however, from this general view, let us see

whether we do not find mention in the Scriptures of particular things that contributed to the joy of our blessed Lord.

1. When we examine the subject on which He had been speaking to His disciples immediately before referring to His joy, we find that it throws important light on this feeling. "As the Father hath loved me, so have I loved you: continue ye in my love. If ye keep my commandments, ye shall abide in my love; even as I have kept the Father's commandments, and abide in his love. These things have I spoken unto you, that my joy might remain in you, and that your joy might be full." He speaks of Himself as abiding in His Father's love, and in immediate connection with this He speaks of His joy. The connection cannot be casual, but must be vital. We note, then, as one ingredient in the joy of Jesus, *the abiding sense of His Fathers love*. He lays stress on the word "abide." He had not mere passing gleams of that love. He abode in it; His soul was bathed in it, as a water plant is bathed in the waters of its pool. And what a blessed source of joy this must have been! The conscious love of any one whom we love and esteem is a source of great joy to us. If at any time we offend him, we are miserable; the thought that he is displeased haunts us, and throws a chill as often as it comes over

us. But when all is made right again, when the old smile is again on his countenance, and the old cordiality in his manner, what a relief we feel!

If, then, the consciousness even of a fellow creature's love can give such joy, what must the consciousness of the love of the infinite God be fitted to bring? And what must it not have brought to Jesus, who knew the Father — knew the infinite glory of His character, and the infinite worth of His love and approval? Doubtless the consciousness of this love was one of the great sources of Christ's strength in carrying on His arduous work. The echoes of these heavenly proclamations, heard at His baptism and at His transfiguration, "This is my beloved Son, in whom I am well pleased," would exert an ever-gladdening influence; and amid all that was sad in the aspect of the world, and awful in the sense of His burden, would diffuse over His spirit an air of contentment, and send Him on His way rejoicing.

2. But if it was a joy for Christ to be loved, it was also a joy for Him to love. "As the Father hath loved me," He said, "so have I loved you." Both things were joyous — to be loved by the Father, and to love His disciples. We note, then, as a second element of Christ's joy, the

exercise of His own gracious, generous, most loving feelings. We have seen that in all the acts and exercises of a holy soul there is a joy like that which attends the play of healthy bodily organs. But there are some exercises of the holy heart that have more of this joy than others. And, in particular, when the heart gushes with a holy love, it is especially rejoicing. Take it the other way. A pinched, fretful, complaining heart cannot be a joyous one. It is a great blessing, many ways, to have a loving heart; not to be easily offended; to be ready to forbear and forgive; ready to help, to pray for, and to bless. Need we say how emphatically this was true of Jesus Christ? "The Spirit of the Lord is upon me; because the Lord hath anointed me to preach good tidings unto the meek; he hath sent me to bind up the broken-hearted, to proclaim liberty to the captives, and the opening of the prison to them that are bound; . . . to comfort all that mourn; to appoint unto them that mourn in Zion, to give unto them beauty for ashes, the oil of joy for mourning, and the garment of praise for the spirit of heaviness."

True, indeed, when the occasion required it. He could be severe and stern. He could knit His brows, and make His voice sound like thunder. "Woe unto thee, Chorazin! woe unto thee, Bethsaida!" "Woe unto you, scribes and

Pharisees, hypocrites! for ye devour widows' houses, and for a pretext make long prayer: therefore ye shall receive the greater damnation." But such judgment was His strange work, and He delighted in mercy. "Come unto me, all ye that labour and are heavy laden, and I will give you rest." "Neither do I condemn thee: go and sin no more." "Father, forgive them; for they know not what they do." "Verily I say unto thee, Today shalt thou be with me in paradise." Such words reveal the deep fountain of lovingkindness there was in the heart of Jesus. A heart thus radiant must have been a heart rejoicing. And the disciples must have known this right well. In the course of His farewell address they often interrupted Him when He said anything that was strange to their minds. But no man interrupted Him when He spoke of His joy. No apostle said to another, What is this that He saith, "That *my joy* might remain in you"? No one asked, What does He mean by His joy? They had seen that amid all His labors and sorrows Jesus had yet a joyful heart; rejoicing in virtue of its own ineffable lovingkindness; rejoicing, as of old, in the habitable parts of His earth, and His delights with the children of men.

Hitherto we have spoken of the joy of Christ in connection with His feelings, and especially the twofold feeling of loving and being loved. But there was a joy connected with His actions as well as His feelings, and to this element we now proceed to advert. And here it may suffice to notice two things: the joy He had in looking back as His work went on — on what He had been enabled to do; and the joy He had in looking forward to the fruit which His work was to bear in the life to come.

3. In the past there was to Him the joy of accomplished work. It was His great privilege to be able to say at the end, "I have finished the work which thou gavest me to do." No true heart can be happy over neglected duty and unfinished work. Even the schoolboy, with all his thoughtlessness, who neglects his tasks, feels in a vague way the pang of reproach, and is humbled at the thought that, instead of controlling his love of play, his love of play has conquered him. Doing one's duty under great trials and difficulties is like fighting a battle; if you stick to duty, and go through with it at all costs, you feel that you have conquered; if you yield to the love of ease or other temptation, you have the sense of being defeated and cast down. It is a great blessing, in this world of hard labor, that it should be so; that there should be something in the very nature of toil successfully borne that carries a reward and a solace; encouraging the weary worker, inspiring him with Gideon's spirit, "faint, yet pursuing." Again and again we

have allusions to this in Scripture. "The joy of harvest" —
what is it but the joy of completed labor; of difficulties
all surmounted; of a campaign successfully carried out?
The shoutings of the builders when the top stone is
placed on the building — what are they but the shouts
of conquerors rejoicing that all the toils and perils of
their undertaking have at length been crowned with the
desired success?

Now if this be true of physical labor, it is true in a higher
sense of labor in the moral and spiritual world. It is the
reward of the good and faithful servant to enter into the
joy of his Lord; and that not merely at the close of his
life, but in a measure at the close of each period of good
and faithful service. That this was pre-eminently our
Lord's experience, many things combine to show us. His
work was very difficult, very constant, very glorious, and
in the end most triumphant. Day by day, we may
believe, as His life passed on, He must have felt the joy
of "something accomplished, something done;" of
powers of body and soul employed for the highest ends;
of temptations conquered; of blessings bestowed on the
needy; of saving truths proclaimed — sent forth on the
wings of parable and metaphor, never to drop their
flight, or cease dropping on the pastures of the
wilderness encouragement and guidance for all weary

souls.

But it was especially as He neared the close of His life that this source of joy appears to have distilled its chief refreshment on Jesus. We find Him, in His intercessory prayer, anticipating by a few hours the approaching close of His life, saying to the Father, "I have glorified thee upon the earth, I have finished the work which thou gavest me to do." Nor was the thought absent from his mind as He hung on the cross. Amid all His anguish there, He knew full well that, ever since His eyes opened on those gray hills of Bethlehem — at least ever since He became conscious of His human existence — He had fulfilled all righteousness, yielded to no temptation, worked the work of Him who sent Him. He had stood patiently in the sinner's room till the last of the bitter waves of punishment due to the sinner had broken over His head. Awfully, indeed, was the sense of victory clouded when, amid the eclipse, the glow of another Sun seemed to be quenched: the Father appeared to have forsaken Him. But ere the close, that sense of desertion had passed away; and the joy that filled His heart, the sense of victory that I thrilled Him, even as He hung on the cross, evinced itself in the loud voice of His dying cry, Tetelestai! — "It is finished!"

4. But if there was a joy in looking back, there was not less a joy in looking forward, and thinking of the unchangeable blessedness to His people in which all His work and sufferings were to end. This is the joy adverted to in the well-known words in the Hebrews: "Looking unto Jesus, the author and finisher of our faith; who *for the joy that was set before him* endured the cross, despising the shame." In the distance He ever saw the mediatorial reward. This was not merely a personal reward, but a reward to be shared by those whom He loved; and the thought of their happiness in sharing it was one of its richest elements. Through the smoke and din of battle, Faith saw the coming triumph. The prisoner who stood before Caiaphas, bound and bleeding, startled his judges by the glory of the vision. "Nevertheless I say unto you, Hereafter shall ye see the Son of man sitting on the right hand of power, and coming in the clouds of heaven." When that vision should be realized, there would be fulfilled all the longings and aspirations of His mediatorial heart. The songs of the angels, rejoicing over repenting sinners, would then pass into the grand hallelujah, to be sung by every creature which is in heaven, and on the earth, and under the earth, and such as are in the sea. Glory everlasting would then redound to the Father. Then, in a world in which sin and sorrow would be for ever unknown, would commence the blessed reign of

holiness and love; souls restored to their orbit would expand in the sunshine of the Father's goodness; and the whole family, bound to each other by ties of holy brotherhood, would find their enjoyment immeasurably heightened by the universal enjoyment around them. Such a vision of the future, rising out of the darkness and confusion of the present, would send a gleam of heaven into the heart of Jesus, and kindle on His countenance a radiance of holy joy.

Such then, as we gather from the Scriptures, are some of the elements of that emotion about which Jesus said, "These things have I spoken unto you, that my joy might remain in you, and that your joy might be full." That they were very precious fountains of joy must be clear to every one who remembers the overwhelming trials and sorrows in the lot of Jesus. Let none of us think the less of Christ's sorrows because they admitted of alleviation (or at least many of them), and gave place in due time to joy. Who can tell the awful bitterness of these sufferings? more especially at those times when the sword of justice seemed to be cutting into His very soul! Yet even the sorrows of Jesus were capable of being lightened by the fountains of joy, the brook by the way, of which it was given Him to drink.

Here, then, is the great lesson for us. If the Man of sorrows found refreshment from these fountains, are they not the fountains that we should prize and resort to? Can we find such fountains elsewhere? Can there be any other waters so fitted to refresh and revive us; so fitted to make us sing as in the days of our youth; to kindle in our souls the fresh feelings of our happiest days? Contrast them with the fountains of mere amusement: how feeble are *their* waters compared to the joys of Christ! The consciousness of the Father's love; the exercise of lovingkindness and all Christian feelings to others; the faithful endeavor, though amid innumerable failures, to do the will of God; the contemplation by faith of the coming glory; are these among the real recreations of our hearts — the exercises that gladden, and refresh, and delight us? Do we often go to Pisgah's top and behold our promised land? Do our feet ever stand on the Delectable Mountains, and our hearts swell as we think of the coming glory? Or is it only to the exciting story, or the amusing exhibition, or the convivial circle that our hearts would go in search of joy?

Alas, if we know nothing better than these, we shall but seek the living among the dead. It is from higher fountains that they are fed who shall "come to Zion with songs and everlasting joy upon their heads: they shall obtain joy and gladness, and sorrow and sighing shall flee away."

For let us mark, ere we close, how Christ indicates that when His joy abides in us our joy is full. " These things have I spoken unto you, that my joy might remain in you, and that your joy might be full." Joy depends much less on what we have, than on what we are. You may give me this and that, and everything that can be thought of, yet raise in my soul no wave of joy. But change me inwardly,' make me like Jesus; let me, like Him, hate wickedness and love righteousness with the whole force of my nature; let me abide, like Him, in the Father's love; let my heart, like His, flow over with loving feelings on every side; let me, like Him, delight in doing God's will, and in finishing, day by day, the work given me to do; let me, like Him, live in expectation of the glory that is to be revealed when He appears with His holy angels, and His redeemed are all gathered from the east and from the west, from the north and from the south; shall not my joy then be pure, deep, and real, a joy unspeakable and full of glory?

The lighter forms of joy, when they involve no sin, need not be banished from our life — bodily recreation, social mirth, lively books and lively conversation. But their place will be secondary; the great fountain will be Christ's fountain. Nay, we will be jealous over ourselves with godly jealousy, lest we so drink of the lighter joys of life as to spoil our relish for the deeper river that makes glad the city of our God.

Fountain of living waters, of which he that drinks shall never thirst again, happy they that dwell beside thee, and drink thy crystal stream! There is gladness in their hearts more than in the time when the corn and wine are most abundant to Others. This, too, it is their privilege to know, that when all life's sorrows are past, and their feet stand within the gates of the New Jerusalem, it is the same joy they shall experience, but in far higher measure, when the Lamb in the midst of the throne shall feed them, and lead them by living fountains of water, and God shall wipe away all tears from their eyes.

HIS PRAYERFULNESS

"He withdrew himself into the wilderness, and prayed."
— Luke 5.16

It is an interesting feature of the third Gospel, that more than any of the other three it dwells on the prayerfulness of our Lord. All of them give prominence to this feature of His earthly life, making it impossible for us even in imagination to separate prayer from the life of Jesus; but many more instances both of His practice of prayer and His exhortations to it are recorded by St. Luke than by the other Evangelists. It is He only that tells us that after His baptism, Jesus was praying: "It came to pass, that Jesus also being baptised, and praying, the heaven was opened" (3.21). It is he only that tells us that after He had cleansed the leper "he withdrew into the wilderness, and prayed" (v. 16). He only informs us that the choice of the twelve apostles followed a night of prayer: "He continued all night in prayer to God. And when it was day, he called unto him his disciples: and of them he chose twelve" (6.12, 13). It is he that tells us that St. Peter's famous confession was made when, as Jesus was alone praying, the disciples came to Him (9.18); and that soon after, when He went up into a mountain, it was "*as he prayed* that the fashion of his countenance changed" (9.29). It is from this Gospel, too, that we learn that the Lord's Prayer was given in answer to a request from one of His disciples, who, when He had ceased praying, said, "Lord, teach us to pray" (11.1). Luke, too, has recorded two parables expressly designed to enforce the duty and privilege of prayer — the parable of the Three Loaves (6.5-8), and the parable of the Importunate Widow (18.1-8). He has recorded also certain memorable instances of true prayer rising from broken hearts, such as the prayer of the publican (18.13) and the prayer of the penitent thief (23.42). And while it was reserved to St. John to record the most striking of all our Lord's own prayers — the intercessory prayer, which forms the very holy of holies of his Gospel — Luke has preserved to us some shorter prayers of infinite beauty and priceless value. Such was His prayer for Peter, that his faith might not fail (22.32), and His prayer for His murderers, "Father, forgive them; for they know not what they do" (23.34). By some this third Gospel has been distinguished as the Gospel of prayer. Certain it is that no one can read it with attention without being struck by the great prominence it gives to the prayerfulness of our Lord.

It is a feature of His life that we might not have looked for beforehand. Had we been left to say, as a matter of speculation, whether a Divine person assuming human nature would practice prayer; whether He would ever be found on His knees, raising the cry of distress, feeling the pressure of unendurable agony, and appealing with strong crying and tears to Him who was able to save Him from death, should we have ventured to say that He would? Beautiful though the prayerfulness of Jesus be in itself, yet when we think who He was, it takes us somewhat by surprise. It is one of the mysteries of godliness, of God manifest in the flesh; yet not a mystery that is quite insoluble; at least, not a mystery that does not, when, pondered, yield very striking lessons, lessons that go to the very heart of our spiritual life.

Why, then, let us ask, did our blessed Lord pray so much? Why, indeed, did He pray at all?

1. The answer of come would be, that He prayed solely

as an example to us. Now, it is certainly true that He did pray as an example to us; and would that we pondered the example, and followed it as we ought! Is it both the duty and the mark of a Christian that he is like Christ? Then on what ground can any one claim to be a Christian who does not pray? Mark the constant prayerfulness of Christ; consider that He hath left us an example that we should follow His steps; and then ask thyself, O prayerless man, On what ground do I claim to be Christ's? You say, perhaps, I am not quite prayerless. I say a few sentences of prayer before I go to bed, and again when I rise in. the morning. But is that really a following of the example of Christ? Had you lived at the same time as He lived, would your practice of hurrying over a few solemn sentences have been a real imitation of Christ's prayerfulness? Would it have justified you in saying, I do as Christ does? Could any one who had never seen the Master at prayer have formed any true conception of His prayers from those of you. His disciple? A copy may, indeed, be a poor and faulty piece of work, but still it is, in some sense, a copy. The lines that a schoolboy writes in his copy book are often a poor, blurred, pitiful contrast to the copperplate line at the top of the page, but still they are in some sense a copy. The grotesque, sprawling letters that, as you would say, ape the difficult curves of the capitals show, by their very awkwardness, how he has tried to follow the original. So, the life of the Christian may be but a poor, blurred, pitiful copy of the life of Christ, but still it is a copy. He tries to be like Jesus; he stretches forth and longs for ability to compass the whole volume of His perfect example. Who among us is honestly trying to be like Christ in this matter of prayerfulness? Who of us tries, in this respect, to honor our Father as much as Christ honored His? "If any man have not the spirit of Christ, he is none of his." That spirit was the spirit of prayer; to be prayerless, therefore, is to be without Christ; and to be without Christ is to be without hope in the world.

2. But while it is true that Christ prayed as an example to us, that is not the whole truth. Indeed, if He had prayed only as an example, it would not have been an example; it would not have been the same exercise of soul; it might have been outwardly similar, but it would have been inwardly different; it would have wanted all that reality and earnestness which is the soul of prayer. If, therefore, Christ's prayers were real prayers, they must have come from that feeling from which all true prayer comes — the feeling of need, the sense of dependence. We enter here on very difficult ground. We touch a question which has exercised theologians for many a century — the relation in which the human nature stood

to the Divine in the person of Jesus Christ. But we do not attempt here to discuss such a question. We content ourselves with the apostle's statement (Philippians 2.7), that though He was in the form of God, and thought it no robbery to be equal with God, He "made himself of no reputation [literally, emptied himself, ἑαυτόν ἐκένωσε] , and took upon him the form of a servant, and was made in the likeness of men." He emptied Himself of His Divine glory in a way to us inscrutable; but so that, as a matter of fact, there was no direct and immediate communication between His necessities as a man and His all-sufficiency as God. He became a true man, assumed all the real properties of manhood.

Now, even of perfect manhood, the sense of dependence is one of the most characteristic features. It is not a mark of human nature in a fallen state only, but even in its state of greatest completeness. Man was made to depend on God as really as the newborn infant depends on its mother, or as the vine depends on the stake that supports it. And Jesus, it appears, was pleased to assume humanity with this, as really as any other feature. He had a man's sense of dependence, a man's feeling of want — of want to be supplied only from the Divine stores, and for the supply of which these stores must be asked in prayer. He had a man's feeling that His soul was not a fountain, but a cistern; and that for all that was needed for His daily life, labors, trials and graces. He must apply to His Father. The fountain from which He drew was the same as ours.

In one point there was a total difference; in other points there was resemblance. He had never to confess sin, or to lament any inward disorder; never to ask, for Himself, medicine to heal or water to cleanse. But for all that was needed to uphold the beauty and purity of His daily life, the Man Christ Jesus had to wait upon the Lord. To enable Him to meet calmly all the venomous attacks of His enemies, to fill His heart with love and His lips with grace, to enable Him to go about doing good, scattering blessings on every side, He had to deal daily with His Father. Had we been beside Him as He was on His knees, we should have heard Him communing with the Father about His work, and pleading for those supplies of bodily strength and mental energy, of wisdom and love and patience, which made His career so blessed. Of the effects of His humiliation, there is none more touching or more beautiful: that He, who in the beginning laid the foundations of the earth, and of whose hands the heavens were the work, should have accepted a relation of dependence that brought Him daily to His knees, impelling him to pray that His human weakness might be strengthened, and all high qualities of soul fostered and ripened for the work given Him to do.

3. But yet again, prayer would go forth from Jesus under the influence of a craving for sympathy and congenial fellowship. Prayer is refreshing as well as strengthening. Human beings engaged in hard and bustling labor need something to revive their spirit in its more subtle energies, especially after discouragement and trial. The bird, when wind and rain have ruffled her plumage, seeks a sheltered nook, that she may not only rest her wing, but trim her feathers; and thus, when the storm is over, be ready for new flights, and songs as blithe as ever. So the spirit of man, ruffled by conflict, needs to be restored and freshened by suitable restoratives.

Now there is no restorative for the weary so effectual as sympathy. How eagerly must the soul of Jesus have longed for it, yet how little of it could He find on earth! Even His chosen disciples did not understand Him, and could not sympathize with Him. One of the most touching cries Christ ever uttered was, "Have not I chosen you twelve, and one of you is a devil?" He could not even approach the most sacred region of His experience, He could not speak of His approaching death, without setting Peter on a strain that drew the reproof, "Get thee behind me, Satan." The memorable scene of the Transfiguration derives its interest, in a large measure, from the fact that of all who were His companions on earth there was net one with whom He could speak "touching the death that he was to accomplish at Jerusalem."

If He wanted sympathy, then. He could not get it from living men. There was no human heart on earth into which He might pour His own. And whatever He might derive from Moses and Elias, that was but a transient gleam — the momentary glow of an angel's visit. But in prayer, in fellowship with the Father, He found, rich and full, the delightful balm for the worn and weary. No man knew the Son but the Father; neither knew any man the Father save the Son, and he to whomsoever the Son should reveal Him. It was impossible that the Father could be indifferent to anything that concerned Him. Well would the Father love to hear the voice of His Son carrying on alone in a bleak world the mightiest and most glorious enterprise in His name, as He told Him of His anxieties, His sorrows, and His difficulties. Sweet would be the sense of sympathy to the harassed soul of Jesus; it would send Him on His way rejoicing; it would shield Him from Elijah's feeling when he fled to the wilderness; it would fit Him for again encountering the scowling Pharisee and the bitter railing of the Sadducee; and it would nerve Him at last for that heroic resolution when, in the full knowledge of the bloody horrors that awaited Him, He set His face steadfastly to go up to Jerusalem.

4. Hence we go on to remark that Jesus prayed because prayer brought the spirit of repose and confidence. We found this remark chiefly on those psalms that are known to express the feelings and experiences of Messiah. Usually they begin with a wail, and as commonly they end with a hallelujah. At the beginning they express the experience of a soul exceeding sorrowful — even unto death; at the close, the triumph of a soul brought up out of a horrible pit, and from the miry clay. At the beginning we see a burdened way-farer, shrinking and shivering under a load too heavy to be borne; at the close, a firm intrepid warrior, who carries his load without trouble, and surveys his foes without fear. And the explanation is that, through prayer, he has been communing with his God. He has been taking his eye off his burdens, his enemies, and his troubles, and fixing it on God, He has been filling his mind with thoughts of the Divine goodness, the Divine love, the Divine promises, the Divine stores of every

kind, and the effect has been more than magical. It has made him that dwelt in dust to awake and sing. It has turned for him his mourning into dancing; it has put off his sackcloth, and girded him with gladness, to the end that his glory might sing praise to God, and not be silent. Who does not know the beginning of the twenty-second Psalm, — what a wail it is? "My God, my God, why hast thou forsaken me?" Who has not noticed how different is its tone near the close, praising the Lord, "for he hath not despised nor abhorred the affliction of the afflicted." And many other Psalms begin and end in a similar way. "How long will thou forget me, O Lord?" is the plaintive opening of the thirteenth. "I will sing unto the Lord, because he hath dealt bountifully with me," is its no less comfortable close. "Deep calleth unto deep at the noise of thy waterspouts; all thy waves and thy billows are gone over me," is the opening burden of the forty-second. "Why art thou cast down, O my soul? and why art thou disquieted within me? hope thou in God, for I shall yet praise him, who is the health of my countenance, and my God," is its exquisitely happy and restful close.

Well must our blessed Lord have known this exquisite effect of believing prayer! It was so precious to Him that, not trusting to what might result from a brief interval of devotion. He sometimes gave Himself up continuously to this employment. "He *withdrew* himself into the wilderness, and prayed." It was not a hurried exercise, even in that busy life Jesus. The proverb says that praying and eating hinder no man. The busiest of Christian workers finds it a good thing, like Luther, to cut a considerable slice out of his busiest day or busiest evening for prayer. Sometimes there are obstacles in our way that, till we have overcome them, prevent us from getting near the throne. But when the wearied and flurried worker *does* get near, it is like breathing the atmosphere of paradise, or bathing in the river of life.

It is this restful and trustful effect of prayer that the lines of Trench express with so much truth and beauty.

Lord, what a change within us one short hour

Spent in Thy presence will prevail to make!

What heavy burdens from our bosom take!

What parched lands refresh as with a shower!

We kneel, and all around us seems to lower;

We rise, and all, the distant and the near,

Stands forth in sunny outline, brave and clear.

We kneel how weak; we rise how full of power;

Why therefore should we do ourselves this wrong.

That we are ever overborne with care?

That we should ever weak or heartless be.

Anxious or troubled, when With us is prayer.

And joy and strength and courage are with Thee?

5. But we should be limiting miserably our Lord's reasons for praying so much, if we thought of His prayers as offered only or mainly for Himself. We have an exquisite specimen of His prayers for others in the seventeenth chapter of John; and we cannot doubt that however much His own necessities may have pressed upon Him, the necessities of others gave emphasis to every prayer. It could not but be so, when all that He asked for Himself had so vital a bearing on the welfare of His people. The prayer just adverted to is an instance in point. It begins with the petition, "Father, glorify thy Son," but as it proceeds, it gathers into its ample bosom those whom the Father had given to the Son; and, widening out still further, it takes in all those also who should believe on Him through their word. What

Christian does not know the delightful glow of enjoyment when in prayer he is enabled in this way to open his heart wider and wider, and bring up to God for His blessing an ever-enlarging company of His fellows? Had we heard Jesus in prayer we should often, doubtless, have found Him thus widening his area of intercession, expanding His supplications till they embraced His people throughout the world, spreading His hands out towards the whole family of man. We should have had light thrown, too, on the wonderful achievement — His continuing all night in prayer to God. We might have found that that was not always the result of a premeditated purpose, but of the delightful feeling that comes from nearness to God. He that gets near the throne, and feels that he has secured the ear of God; he that knows that his Father is registering his requests, and that is almost sensible of the warm glow of God's countenance, will be in no haste to leave this third heaven of communion. Topic suggests topic, intercession genders intercession, till the whole field of the kingdom is embraced: his prayer spreads from sea to sea, and from the river to the ends of the earth. His feeling resembles that of the prophet's wife, when the pot of oil in her house was so multiplied that it seemed as if it would flow forever; so that she was fain to fill not only every vessel in her own house, but all the vessels of her neighbors, and, as we may believe, was disappointed when her son told her that there was not one more vessel to fill. There are times at the throne of grace, when the stream of blessing seems to flow so as to suffice not for ourselves only, but for our families, for our friends, for our Church, for public interests of every kind — enough to fill every empty vessel that can be brought to the stream. Men often ridicule long prayers, and when prayers are made long on the pretext of sanctity they deserve the ridicule; but prayer prolonged in secret because the oil is multiplying and the assurance is given of a blessing that there is not room enough to contain — that, doubtless, is like Christ's all-night prayer; it is prayer without the sense of weariness; it is prayer that brings down the very elixir of life, the very abundance of heaven.

Is it necessary to make any formal application of a subject so well calculated to apply itself? We have seen that, in large measure, the great prayerfulness of Jesus arose from the human feeling of dependence, from His sense of need. Who can be at a loss to draw the inference? If Jesus felt His dependence, His need of daily stores from heaven, how much more cause have we to feel the same? If He, with His sinless nature, needed to pray, how much more we, shapen in iniquity and conceived in sin? If He needed it, in whom the prince of this world could find nothing, how much more we to whom he find access through every organ of our body — we might almost say through every pore of our skin? If He needed it, without one besetting sin, how much more we who are so troubled by the law in our members that wars against the law of our mind, and brings us into captivity to the law of sin in our members? If He needed it, who had devoted Himself heart and soul to the Father's work and the Father's will, how much more we who are so prone to unworthy compromises with our own inclinations, and who have such constant occasion to cry out, "Iniquities prevail against us"? Is this not a valid argument? Is there any resisting the conclusion that it befits us to "continue in prayer;" nay, even to "pray without ceasing"?

There can be no vigorous Christian life without prayer. Such of us as pray little too plainly show this. We content ourselves with a few general, and somewhat formal petitions, and what follows? We go into the world, but instead of imparting a Christian tone to the world, the world gives a secular tone to us; temptation comes, and we are basely defeated; opportunities of doing good come, but we try not to improve them; difficulties come, and we are worried; trials come, and we are fretful; we lay our plans without asking God's counsel; we become worldly, selfish, unbelieving; a blight comes over us; we fade like the leaves of autumn. And the prayers we do offer, of what quality are they? Where is the ladder between earth and heaven with the angels of God ascending and descending? Where are the glowing thanksgivings for prayer heard and mercies bestowed? If once it was different with us, how great has been our fall, and how urgent is the summons from our Lord: "Remember therefore from whence thou art fallen, and repent, and do the first works; or else I will come unto thee quickly, and will remove thy candlestick out of his place, except thou repent."

It has been said often and truly, that backsliding begins in the closet. It is at the closet door that Delilah lies in wait for Samson; well knowing that if she can prevent him from entering there, she may soon have him asleep on her lap, her scissors will be applied to his locks, and he will be weak as other men. Let us guard our closets from the arts of every Delilah. Let us see to it that nothing robs us of our seasons of secret prayer. Let us beware of the pleas of weariness at night and hurry in the morning; let us beware of the tempting book, the magazine, the newspaper, the story that greedily steals our last waking moment, and leaves neither time nor heart for the Bible nor for prayer. Let us tell God of all that concerns us. Let us ask Him for every thing we need. Let us spread before Him the sins we must overcome, the duties we must fulfill, the temptations we have to meet, and the graces we ought to manifest. Let us tell Him how we need from Him light and love, faith and trust, peace and purity. Let us commune with Him about our friends, our unconverted relations, and such as are especially in the way of temptation; and let our prayers widen out to take in our neighborhood, our country, our race — all that stand in need of God's mercy and blessing.

And if we thus value prayer in secret, we shall be the more ready to prize opportunities of social and public prayer. We shall be delighted to have others backing us in our wrestlings, and we shall have a deeper assurance of the efficacy of the process. We shall come to fed that in reply to these unseen but earnest traffickings with heaven there comes down to us a real wealth, the most precious of all treasures; the time is not wasted, but leads to glorious gain — gain more glorious than if we carried away from the mercy-seat handfuls of literal gold; seeing that what we get is not the gold that perisheth, but the treasures of heaven, where neither moth nor rust doth corrupt, nor thieves break through and steal.

Does any reader's conscience smite him? Does it say, You have lived a prayerless life, most unlike to the life of Jesus, and have never drawn near in earnest to the throne of grace? Does the discovery make him miserable, and impatient of the great gulf he sees yawning between him and God? Is he fain to cross the gulf? Let him draw near by that new and living way which Christ hath consecrated for us, and he will reach the holiest of all. And that blessed Master, to whom the disciples appealed for their lesson in prayer, will prove to him, too, a most willing and kind instructor. He will pour out on him the spirit of grace and supplication, and show him how truly it is written that "through him we all have access by one Spirit unto the Father."

HIS ENDURING OF THE CROSS

"Father, the hour is come." — John 17.1

We do not know when "the shadow of the cross" first fell on Christ; but we do know that during the latter part of His public ministry, at all events, the thought of it haunted Him like a specter. There was a crisis of His life, so peculiar in the horrors it was to bring, that it stood out in dark relief from every other part of it; and as often as it presented itself to His thoughts, a horror of great darkness came upon Him. As we have seen, He thought and spoke of it as emphatically "the hour" (Matthew 26.45; Mark 14.35; Luke 22.53; John 7.30; 8.20; 12.23; 13.1; 17.1) thus, denoting on the one hand its marked, well-defined character; and indicating, on the other, that its duration was to be short — a brief season of unprecedented trial. We have seen that the thought of this crisis was so terrible, that at times the soul of Jesus shrunk from it; and that it was necessary for Him to rally His courage by agonies of prayer ere He was able to compose Himself to bear it. It was this hour that showed Jesus in His noblest aspect. Even in the case of men, it is usually some great trial that reveals the depths of their character, bringing out their strongest qualities. In the case of Jesus, the revelation of character in this crisis of His life was wonderfully glorious; never, at any other time, are we so constrained to say, "Thou art fairer than the children of men!"

Two simple inquiries are suggested in reference to this crisis; in the first place, To what was it due? and secondly, What was there in our Lord's conduct in it that especially exemplified His spirit and character?

1. As to the cause of the crisis; the Christian church, with almost unbroken harmony, has refused to regard it as springing from merely outward causes. It is quite true that the crucifixion, with all its attendant horrors, and in the case of Jesus with all the suffering that preceded it, was a most harrowing ordeal, and well fitted to produce an intense recoil. Still, there was no reason why even this prospect should have affected Jesus so profoundly, for martyrs and patriots have often been strengthened

to face such tortures without flinching. This Church has invariably concluded that the recoil of Jesus from "the hour" was connected with His peculiar position as the sin-bearer, "the Lamb of God that taketh away the sin of the world." Without attempting to open up all the grounds for this conclusion, it may suffice for us here to draw attention to two passages from the Old Testament, which Jesus repeated in reference to the crisis, each very significant in itself, but doubly significant in the connection in which they stand in their original places.

The first is recorded by St, Luke (22.37): it is a quotation from the fifty-third chapter of Isaiah, made by our Lord in these terms: "For I say unto you that this that is written must yet be accomplished in me. And he was reckoned among the transgressors: for the things concerning me have an end." Evidently our Lord meant that the accomplishment of this prediction was the great matter that stood between that moment and the completion of all that was written concerning Him. Now the significance of this prediction can be seen only by studying attentively the chapter where it occurs. The very point of that chapter is this, that whereas the sufferings of Messiah had the appearance of being inflicted by men, in a deeper sense they were laid on Him by God. To be reckoned among transgressors by man would not have been very terrible to Christ; but to be reckoned among transgressors by His Father was a peculiar and very awful trial. This treatment as a sinner was what turned the heart of Jesus; not the fact of His being falsely represented by unjust men as a malefactor; but the fact of His having to bear the doom of a sinner, in all its most appalling elements, at the hand of the holy Judge and Ruler of all.

Let us try to bring this out more clearly. And for this purpose, let us go with the crowd to Calvary, and survey the scene that falls there under our eye.

On the very first glance we are struck by one thing — the absence of all that is pleasant, beautiful, and refreshing to the senses; and the presence of everything ugly, atrocious, revolting. Everything about the place has an odious look. There is no attempt at order or decency. Skulls and bones, tufts of hair and putrid flesh, are scattered about. The three crosses, dingy and blood-stained, supporting three naked bodies, ghastly and blood-stained too, are but in keeping with their surroundings. And the moral spectacle is of a piece with the physical. Every insult is heaped on the person of Jesus. The soldiers, the spectators, the priests and elders in their robes of holy office, seem to vie with each other in insulting Him. In all the gatherings, there is but one voice raised on His behalf, and that is the voice of the robber at His side. The pure-minded women and even the disciples who love Him so well, cowed and horrified, stand afar off (Luke 23.49). He seems an alien from His Father's house; His friends and brethren have forsaken His fellowship. And as He is forsaken of man, so He seems to be of God. The sun becomes dark, and will not shine on Him. The face of the Father seems darkened likewise; and it too refuses to shine.

What means this extraordinary sight? It means that Jesus of Nazareth has been "reckoned among the transgressors." It means that He is bearing the true doom and desert of sin. It is the cross telling us what happened to Jesus when He took the sinner's place, and underwent the sinner's doom. It is the cross proclaiming how the sinner deserves to be cast forth into an unclean place, with every vile and noisome influence around him; driven beyond the reach of every bright and refreshing scene; separated from the fellowship of all good and loving beings; abandoned to the cruel hands of the most ungodly and merciless; deserted by the very sun that cannot let his bright beams fall on him; forsaken even by God, who can neither relieve the agonies of His body nor soothe the anguish of His mind. The unclean place, the unrestrained passions of the mob, the unmitigated sufferings of soul and body, the coldness of God, the chill touch of death — what were these but the great elements of the doom of sin? Sin drives the bearer of it outside the holy city, outside all that is bright and genial, into a scene of filth and disorder; away from the light of heaven, away from the smile of God, away from the sympathy of man, into the region of darkness and curses, and passion and cruelty and death. This was what Jesus suffered when the word that had been written of Him was accomplished, "He was reckoned among the transgressors." This it was that made His sorrow like to no other sorrow.

The other very significant word is from the twenty-second Psalm; "My God, my God, why hast thou forsaken me?" The use of this word implies that in His hour of utmost need Jesus felt Himself bereft of a fellowship which He had ever been wont to enjoy, and that the sense of this bereavement was the very climax of His suffering. It indicates the desolation and consternation of a soul that during a lifetime of troubles ever had one true friend to fall back on; but now, in its extremest need, is forsaken by that last and only comforter! The concentrated bitterness of this experience was equal to unnumbered years of pain. It was this that gave to "the hour" its most oppressive and unendurable feature; as if all the bitterness of hell and all the anguish of eternity had been squeezed into its little span!

2. Without lingering more on this, let us proceed to the other subject of inquiry; let us consider what light His behavior in this terrible crisis threw on the spirit and character of our blessed Lord.

1. First, it illustrated His resolute purpose to bear everything that was implied in the office of Messiah. In no other connection do we find Him so often using the word "must," to repel considerations of an opposite kind. At Caesarea Philippi He told His disciples that He "*must* go to Jerusalem . . . and be killed." "This that is written," He said, "*must* yet be accomplished in me." "How then shall the scripture be fulfilled that thus it *must* be?" If in Gethsemane He seemed to take another view, and to doubt the absolute necessity of such sufferings, evidently it was but one part of His nature that recoiled; His deeper purpose was to face the storm. This heroic devotion of His to the duties of His office — to the duties of an office which He had taken

spontaneously on Him — is the most remarkable exhibition of virtue ever given in human form.

In no man by whom this great fact in Christ's history is really taken in can a slumbering conscience be found. For who can see the Savior that loved him and gave Himself for him paying such unprecedented homage to, the will of God, without being impelled to fling from him all the sophistries of his deceitful heart, renounce the pleasures of self-indulgence, and stand firm and steadfast on the rock of duty?

But while the resolute purpose of our Lord exemplified His devotion to duty, it showed not less clearly the triumph of His love. For in this case duty was the offspring of love; love undertook the obligation; and all through His life, and especially at its close, love and duty went hand in hand. At the end, the triumph of love was all the greater, because the wickedness it had to conquer was so frightful. Cold floods fell upon a warm heart, but the heart remained as warm as ever. At Calvary, men seemed to defy the love of Christ. They did every conceivable thing to turn it into hatred. But the endurance of Christ showed that no impression had been made on it. His was love that many waters could not quench, and that floods could not drown.

It is indeed a love that passeth knowledge. The most loving hearts feel that baffles them, and that their best returns

Our delight

Is watching the dear love poured out to Thee

From ever fuller chalice. Blessed they

Who love Thee more than we do.

2. Again, we mark in Christ, even under the shadow of this great trial, a very wonderful composure, enabling Him to give attention to the many momentous matters that, in succession. demanded His notice. All through His life, indeed, we find our Lord marked by a marvelous orderliness and business-like composure of mind. One thing was never allowed to jostle another, however full He might be of projects, and however pressed by anxieties. And as the crisis of His suffering approached, this orderliness and composure became more wonderful. There are instances familiar to most of us in

private life, of persons in great agony entering calmly into the details of business, or of persons when dying giving directions for their funeral, and the arrangements of the family, down to the minutest particular. But no such instance approaches the composure and deliberate forethought of our blessed Lord. At the approach of the Passover he describes minutely to the two disciples what they were to do in preparation for it. Assembled with the Twelve, he deliberately girds himself, pours water into a basin, washes the feet of the disciples, deals with the objections of Peter, explains the import of the act, and enforces the example which it supplies. With equal calmness He institutes the most solemn ordinance of the Christian religion, the holiest of Christian mysteries; giving utterance to the few but ever memorable words which were to be repeated by His whole Church, on the most solemn occasions, until He should come again. Then with a courage which none can know but those whose duty it has been to break in on the serene joy of a friendly company by some startling and horrible announcement, He exposes the treachery of Judas. With equal firmness He rebukes the confidence of Peter. If any documents in the world bear the stamp of repose, it is the farewell discourse and the intercessory prayer. But the agony in the garden shows us through what great conflicts that self-possession was maintained. Like some basaltic crag which, cropping up at a single spot, gives evidence of a great chain of rock below, the prayer in the garden gives evidence of an underlying habit of prayer, the habit of His life, through which our Lord maintained His habitual serenity, and went on steadily with His work. How precious is the store of tranquil energy to which these footsteps of our Lord point us; and how much more might we not all accomplish in the short span of a lifetime if we sought it as He did, and came from it with our spirits composed and fortified like His!

3. But indeed all the highest qualities of the human nature of Christ shone out with pre-eminent luster in the crisis of His sufferings. In the case even of mere men we sometimes find the graces that have marked their life brightening out into peculiar splendor when they are dying. But this is especially true of Christ. Do we admire in His life the meekness that was never ruffled amid the plots and calumnies of His enemies? How bright was that quality when hosts of false witnesses were uttering their lies against Him; when the Roman governor taunted Him with His silence; and when the high priest and his associates mocked His most solemn words. Do we admire in His life the self-denying patience that would not turn the stones of the wilderness into bread? that would not create figs on the fig-tree to break His

morning fast? that bore with all the stupidity of His disciples, and calmly waited till God's time should come for vindicating His claims? How signally was that spirit shown at the last, when a prayer to the Father might have brought to His aid more than twelve legions of angels, and when all the taunts of the bystanders could not induce Him to come down from the cross. What self-denying patience was there in His bearing all the accumulated horrors of the crucifixion. When did the spirit of forgiveness reach such a climax as in His prayer for His murderers? When did His beneficence rise so high as in His promise to the thief?

But there is one quality of Christ's demeanor on the cross that, owing to the most unfavorable situation for it, arrests especial attention — His majesty. We know that with all His humility there was habitually an air of native majesty about Christ that proclaimed Him to be more than man. But the crowning humiliation of the cross, the exposure of the naked body, and all the other indignities of the situation, seemed sure to prove fatal to a majestic bearing. Yet see how Jesus rises above all! In that condition which tempts men to think of Him as a worm, and no man, He manifests a purity of soul, a holy trust in God, a gentle and forgiving love to man, and a calm dignity of demeanor, enough, had there been no earthquake, to make the centurion exclaim, "Truly this was the Son of God!"

4. Still another feature of Christ's character, exemplified by His behavior in the crisis of His suffering, is His satisfaction in the completion of His work. That cry with a loud voice, "It is finished," immediately before he resigned His spirit into His Father's hands, was in many ways most significant. It indicated the feeling of the Redeemer surveying His work from the close, corresponding to the feeling of the Creator when He saw everything He had made, and, behold, it was very good. It showed our Lord's delight in finished work. Things half done, or done hastily and superficially, were things that He could not bear. There is a finish about every proverb, every illustration He ever uttered, that indicates His love for finished work. His miracles were complete miracles, His cures were entire cures, His conversions were whole conversions. Doubtless, if we had seen His work in the carpenter's shop at Nazareth, we should have found that no slim, half-finished work ever left His hands. And now this feature of His character, exemplified through life in smaller things, appears in connection with the great work of redemption. He surveys that work and sees it complete, and a gleam of satisfaction lights up His dying

face. No painter has ever caught it; no picture of the crucifixion represents the joy of His heart on the survey of the completed work, triumphing over all His agonies. But the kindling eye showed that it was there, and the tones of that ringing voice, that sounded so unexpectedly above all the din of Calvary, "It is finished!"

Death upon His face

Is rather shine than shade,

A tender shine by looks beloved made;

He seemeth dying in a quiet place,

And less by iron wounds in hands and feet,

Than heart-broke by new joy too sudden and too sweet.

There were few that understood the word as it was spoken. But emphatically it has proved to be a word that liveth and abideth for ever. To many a burdened soul, wearied with the effort to work out a righteousness of its own, the discovery of the finished work of Jesus has been a glorious revelation from heaven. It has set their feet upon a rock, and put a new song in their mouths. It has been a strong tower lo them through life, where peace and safety have been found. And in death, even when in deep abasement on account of their sin, it has given them a hope full of immortality, and a joy unspeakable and full of glory.

HIS DYING WORD

"Father, into thy hands I commend my spirit." — Luke 23.46

We are told that before He uttered these words Jesus cried with a loud voice. The cry with a loud voice could not have been other than the word recorded by St. John: "It is finished." After uttering that word with a loud voice, Jesus seems to have said more softly, "Father, into thy hands I commend my spirit," and immediately to have given up the ghost. The one word was spoken to the world, and therefore uttered in a loud voice; the other was whispered, as it were, to the Father, and therefore was probably heard by much fewer persons. The one word, as has been said, was His last greeting to earth; the other was His first greeting to heaven. We are now to consider Christ's password, as it were, to heaven — the word on which He flung Himself into the dread gulf, so dark and fathomless to the eye of sense.

In a sense, this last word is not His own; it is quoted from the Psalms. "A text of Scripture was the torch that lighted Him into the valley of the shadow of death." When we examine the psalm from which it is quoted (the thirty-first) we are a little surprised. The psalm is not about death. It is about enemies who were persecuting the Psalmist during his lifetime, and it was that He might be delivered from them that he committed his soul into the hands of God. It is therefore a prayer which David offered in the ordinary course of his life. And David being a type of Christ, and his feelings and experiences corresponding in some measure with Christ's, the prayer was probably one which Christ too offered in the ordinary course of His life. Probably it was not the first time that Christ used the words as a prayer for Himself. In the case of Christ, as in the case of His followers, there was not the difference that many suppose between the struggles of life and the struggle of death. The experience characteristic of the one is not wholly unlike to that which is characteristic of the other. In a sense, every true Christian dies daily. There is a habit of committing the soul into God's hands to be practiced daily, and if it be thus practiced, we shall feel nothing very strange when we are called to do it for the last time. It is those who know nothing of the habit while living, that find it so difficult to do the thing when dying. There, as in other things, to begin early is to end well.

Let us examine with care this last prayer of our Lord's. He commits His spirit into His Father's hands, as feeling that He is utterly unable to take care of it Himself. Does not this show how truly He was made like unto His brethren? He showed that sense of utter helplessness which all, except the most reckless of men, experience in the article of death. A universal instinct tells us that we are helpless then. Our spirits, severed from our bodies, will be at the mercy of circumstances which we cannot control. If ever we need to have a friend awaiting us at the end of a journey, it is surely at the end of that journey. If the infant Moses in his ark of bulrushes needed help, not less do we when our souls float on the waters of Jordan. Even though in the same person Jesus was Son of God as well as Son of man, yet as man the moment of utter helplessness came upon Him. It is the moment when the human spirit feels most deeply its need of God. And in that moment His prayer is, "Father, into thy hands I commend my spirit."

But as there is a sense of helplessness here, so also

there is a feeling of confidence. Father, says Christ; and as He says, so He feels; I can trust Thy fatherly heart. What Thou mayest do with Me, whither Thou mayest conduct Me, what new experience of life may await Me, I do not inquire. All that I leave at Thy disposal. It will be all right. "Into thy hands I commend my spirit."

This serene confidence of the man Christ Jesus was not the result of a mere transient experience. As we have said, He had been in the constant habit of commending His spirit into the hands of His Father. He had often felt a helplessness and loneliness which compelled Him to do so. In the presence of all His trials, duties, and perplexities, this had been His habit. Now He is about to pass through the gate of death. But the same protection will avail here as at other times. "Father, into thy hands I commend my spirit."

The word with which Jesus passed into the unseen world has proved a precious password for many who have gone after Him. The first Christian martyr but slightly modified it: "Lord Jesus, receive my spirit." Noble John Huss of Bohemia quickly repelled the anathema. of his murderers by means of it, when he was condemned to be burnt, and when, in token of his degradation from the priestly office, seven bishops put on his head a cap painted with figures of devils and inscribed with the word "arch-heretic," and proceeded to say, "Now we deliver thy soul to Satan." "But I," said the martyr, "commend it into Thy hands, O Jesus Christ, for Thou hast redeemed it." Young James Renwick, in the like circumstances, on the scaffold at the Grassmarket of Edinburgh, uttered the same words just as he was turned over the ladder. Luther died with them on his lips. Nor have they been serviceable only to martyrs and confessors. One, at least, of the world's intellectual giants laid hold of them, when contemplating his coming death. "I commend my soul," writes Shakespeare, in his last will and testament, "into the hands of God my Creator, hoping, and assuredly believing, through the only merits of Jesus Christ my Saviour, to be a partaker of life everlasting." Happy they who can calmly make this disposal of their spirit. For failing this, what shadow of an alternative can we find?

The dying word of our Lord acquires a new significance, if, with some, we can regard it as spoken by Him in His representative capacity. For did He not represent His people on the cross? Was He not the head of the body of which they are members? and in commending His own spirit to the Father, did He not virtually commend theirs too? Was He not bespeaking the gracious protection of the Highest not for Himself only, but for all that the Father had given Him? What a blessed truth to fall back on, if at any time we shiver at the thought of the grave! It is not as if no provision had been made for us, and no one were engaged to meet us on the other side. He who is to say at the last reckoning, "Inasmuch as ye did it to the least of these my brethren, ye did it unto me," holds to the same principle in His dealings with the Father. It is the same thing to receive the spirits of His people as to receive His own; and the prayer that sought and secured the one, sought and secured the other also.

But let us all take up the prayer of Christ for ourselves likewise, and commit our spirits to His protection both in life and in death. Am I going out into the world to do my business, to transact with my fellows, to be encompassed with temptations to passion, greed, selfishness, harshness, guile? Father, into Thy hands I commend my spirit. Guide and guard it as Thou wouldst have it; and in all the turmoil and temptation of business, help me to walk as Thy child.

Am I going to know adversity and sorrow? Is sickness coming on me, or loss of goods, or some other cross hard to bear? Father, into Thy hands I commend my spirit. Make it meek, patient, happy, holy; like the sandal-tree, emitting more fragrance the more it is riven; like the musk-plant, richer in perfume by being bruised.

Is it my destiny to prosper and be exalted? Am I to rise in the world, and become an object of honor and regard? Father, into Thy hands I commend my spirit. Leave it not to be shriveled and pulverized by worldly influences; let Thy rain and dew still fall upon it; keep me loyal to Thee, mindful of my pilgrim state, humble in all my feelings, ready to distribute, willing to communicate.

Am I disposed to a life of usefulness? Do I recognize my duty not to live to myself; and, under that conviction, do I undertake service for my Lord? Father, into Thy hands I commend my spirit. Keep me 'from offensive presumption and spiritual pride, from hard and uncharitable dealing with others; make me learn of Him who was meek and lowly, that I may serve Thee in the true spirit of Thy Son, and remember that in His kingdom the servant of all is the greatest of all.

Am I going to sleep? Is my spirit to be set loose, to roam as it pleases, while conscience, its under-keeper, is taking rest in unconsciousness? Father, into Thy hands I commend my spirit; keep Thine eye on it in its wanderings; may no impure thought find entrance to it; may its course be upward, toward the regions of light;

For in my dreams I'd be

Nearer, my God, to Thee,

Nearer to Thee!

Finally, am I going to die? Am I to encounter the dark gulf from which our instincts shrink? Is the earthly house of the tent going to be taken down? And after death, cometh the judgment? And then the holy city, and the near beholding of God? Father, into Thy hands I commend my spirit. Shepherd of Israel, gather me in Thine arms and carry me in Thy bosom over the swelling Jordan; accept me and acquit me in the judgment. And not me only. Into Thy hands I commend the spirits of my near and dear ones, my flesh and blood, and of my neighbors and friends and foes. Care for them all. Take hold of them, make them Thy faithful servants and loving children; and when their days come that they shall die, let an entrance be ministered to them abundantly into the everlasting kingdom of our Lord and Savior Jesus Christ.

Made in United States
North Haven, CT
17 January 2022